THE INTOLERABLE GOD

The Intolerable God

Kant's Theological Journey

Christopher J. Insole

WILLIAM B. EERDMANS PUBLISHING COMPANY
GRAND RAPIDS, MICHIGAN / CAMBRIDGE, U.K.

Published 2016 by
Wm. B. Eerdmans Publishing Co.
2140 Oak Industrial Drive N.E., Grand Rapids, Michigan 49505 /
P.O. Box 163, Cambridge CB3 9PU U.K.

Printed in the United States of America

22 21 20 19 18 17 16   7 6 5 4 3 2 1

Library of Congress Cataloging-in-Publication Data

Names: Insole, Christopher J., author.
Title: The intolerable God : Kant's theological journey / Christopher J. Insole.
Description: Grand Rapids, Michighan : Eerdmans Publishing Company, 2016. |
Includes index.
Identifiers: LCCN 2016007367 | ISBN 9780802873057 (pbk. : alk. paper)
Subjects: LCSH: Kant, Immanuel, 1724-1804. — Religion.
Classification: LCC B2799.R4 I57 2016 | DDC 230.092 — dc23
LC record available at http://lccn.loc.gov/2016007367

www.eerdmans.com

Contents NB- 82F n·}}at !

Acknowledgments

I give thanks to Nigel Biggar, and to the McDonald Centre for Theology, Ethics & Public Life at the University of Oxford, for the opportunity to give the 2013 McDonald Lectures, upon which this book is based. I am grateful for feedback received after these lectures, and at the roundtable discussion that followed the completion of the lecture series, with formal responses from Terrence Irwin, Adrian Moore, and Keith Ward.

Thanks to David Dwan, Ben DeSpain, and Nathaniel Warne for comments and advice on earlier drafts of the book, and to Jon Pott, long-time Editor in Chief at Eerdmans, for his enthusiasm for the project. I thank my parents for all their support, nurture, and encouragement of my endeavors, intellectual and otherwise.

This book is dedicated to Lisa Maria Insole, my wife, in gratitude for the surprising shared enjoyment we had in drafting the lectures that became this book.

Method of Citation

All items marked with an asterisk are part of the Cambridge Edition of the Works of Immanuel Kant. Numbers following listings are volume and page numbers in the standard German (Akademie) edition of Kant.

A/B   Citations to the first *Critique* are to the A (first edition) or B (second edition) pages. *Critique of Pure Reason (CPR)*. Edited and translated by Paul Guyer and Allen W. Wood. Cambridge: Cambridge University Press, 1998.*

APV   *Anthropologie in pragmatischer Hinsicht* (1798). In *Anthropology, History, and Education.* Edited and translated by Robert B. Louden and Günter Zöller. Cambridge: Cambridge University Press, 2008.* 7: 117-333.

CHH   *Mutmaßlicher Anfang der Menschengeschichte* (1786). *Conjectures on the Beginning of Human History.* In *Kant: Political Writings.* Second Enlarged Edition. Edited by Hans Reiss. Translated by H. B. Nisbet. Cambridge: Cambridge University Press, 1991. 8: 107-23.

CJ   *Kritik der Urtheilskraft* (1790). *Critique of the Power of Judgment.* Edited by Paul Guyer. Translated by Paul Guyer and Eric Matthews. Cambridge: Cambridge University Press, 2000.* 5: 167-484.

Coll   "Moral Philosophy: Collins' Lecture Notes" (1784-85). In *Lectures on Ethics.* Translated by Peter Heath. Edited by J. B. Schneewind and Peter Heath. Cambridge: Cambridge University Press, 2001.*

Corr   *Correspondence* (1749-1800). In *Correspondence.* 10: 7–12: 370.

CPrR   *Kritik der praktischen Vernunft* (1788). *Critique of Practical Reason.* In *Practical Philosophy.* Translated and edited by Mary J. Gregor. Cambridge: Cambridge University Press, 2008.* 5: 3-309.

D   *Träme eines Geistersehers, erläutert durch Träume der Metaphysik* (1766). *Dreams of a Spirit-Seer Elucidated by Dreams of Metaphysics.* In *Theoretical Philosophy, 1755-1770.* Translated and edited by David Walford and Ralf Meerbote. Cambridge: Cambridge University Press, 1992.* 2: 317-73.

DR   *Danziger Rationaltheologie* (1784). 28: 1231-1319.

DFW   *Declaration concerning Fichte's Wissenschaftslehre* (1799). In *Correspondence.* 12:370-71.

E   Kant's notes on his copy of the *Critique of Pure Reason.* In Benno Erdmann, *Nachträge zu Kants Kritik der reinen Vernunft.* Kiel: Lipsius & Ticher, 1881.

EaT   *Das Ende aller Dinge* (1794). *The End of All Things.* In *Religion and Rational Theology.* Translated and edited by Allen W. Wood and George di Giovanni. Cambridge: Cambridge University Press, 1996.* 8: 328-39.

GW   *Grundlegung zur Metaphysik der Sitten* (1786). *Groundwork of the Metaphysics of Morals.* In *Practical Philosophy.* Translated and edited by Mary J. Gregor. Cambridge: Cambridge University Press, 2008.* 4: 385-463.

ID   *De mundi sensibilis atque intelligibilis forma et principiis* (1770). *Concerning the Form and Principles of the Sensible and Intelligible World* [*Inaugural Dissertation*]. In *Theoretical Philosophy, 1755-1770.* Translated and edited by David Walford and Ralf Meerbote. Cambridge: Cambridge University Press, 1992.* 2: 385-419.

JL   *Jäsche Logic.* In *Lectures on Logic.* Translated and edited by J. Michael Young. Cambridge: Cambridge University Press, 2004.* 9: 1-150.

LPE   *Vorlesung über die philosophische Encylopädie.* 29: 8-12.

LPed   *Lectures on Pedagogy* (1803). In *Anthropology, History, and Education.* Edited and translated by Robert B. Louden and Günter Zöller. Cambridge: Cambridge University Press, 2008.* 9: 437-99.

LPR   *Philosophische Religionslehre nach Pölitz* (1783-84). *Lectures on the Philosophical Doctrine of Religion.* In *Religion and Rational Theology.* Translated and edited by Allen W. Wood and George

di Giovanni. Cambridge: Cambridge University Press, 1996.*
28: 993-1126.

MD   *Metaphysik Dohna* (1792). In *Lectures on Metaphysics*. Translated and edited by Karl Ameriks and Steve Naragon. Cambridge: Cambridge University Press, 1997.* 28: 656-90.

MetM   *Die Metaphysik der Sitten* (1797). *The Metaphysics of Morals*. In *Practical Philosophy*. Translated and edited by Mary J. Gregor. Cambridge: Cambridge University Press, 2008.* 6: 203-430.

MK₂   *Metaphysik K₂* (early 1790s). 28: 709-816.

ML₁   *Metaphysik L₁* (1790). In *Lectures on Metaphysics*. Translated and edited by Karl Ameriks and Steve Naragon. Cambridge: Cambridge University Press, 1997.* 28: 195-301.

NE   *Principiorum primorum cognitionis metaphysicae nova delucidatio* (1755). *New Elucidation of the First Principles of Metaphysical Cognition*. In *Theoretical Philosophy, 1755-1770*. Translated and edited by David Walford and Ralf Meerbote. Cambridge: Cambridge University Press, 1992.* 1: 385-487.

NTV   *Natürliche Theologie Volckmann* (1783). 28: 1131-1225.

Ob   *Beobachtungen über das Gefühl des Schönen und Erhabenen* (1764-65). *Notes on Observations on the Feeling of the Beautiful and Sublime*. In *Notes and Fragments*. Edited by Paul Guyer. Translated by Curtis Bowman, Paul Guyer, and Frederick Rauscher. Cambridge: Cambridge University Press, 2005.* 2: 205-55.

OD   *On a Discovery whereby Any New Critique of Pure Reason Is Sure to Be Made Superfluous by an Older One*. In *Theoretical Philosophy after 1781*. Cambridge: Cambridge University Press, 2004.*

OIT   *Was heisst. Sich im Denken orientiren?* (1786). *What Does It Mean to Orient Oneself in Thinking?* In *Religion and Rational Theology*. Translated and edited by Allen W. Wood and George di Giovanni. Cambridge: Cambridge University Press, 1996.* 8: 133-46.

OP   *Opus Postumum* (1786-1803). Translated and edited by Eckart Förster and Michael Rosen. Cambridge: Cambridge University Press, 1998.* 21:9–22:452.

OPA   *Der einzig mögliche Beweisgrund zu einer Demonstration des Daseins Gottes* (1763). *The Only Possible Argument in Support of a Demonstration of the Existence of God*. In *Theoretical Phi-*

losophy, 1755-1770. Translated and edited by David Walford and Ralf Meerbote. Cambridge: Cambridge University Press, 1992.* 2: 63-163.

PP   *Zum ewigen Frieden. Ein philosophischer Entwurf* (1795). *Toward Perpetual Peace: A Philosophical Sketch.* In *Practical Philosophy.* Translated and edited by Mary J. Gregor. Cambridge: Cambridge University Press, 2008.* 8: 341-86.

Pr   *Prolegomena zu einer jeden künftigen Metaphysik, die als Wissenschaft wird auftreten können* (1783). *Prolegomena to Any Future Metaphysics That Will Be Able to Come Forward as Science.* In *Theoretical Philosophy after 1781.* Edited by Henry Allison and Peter Heath. Translated by Gary Hatfield, Michael Friedman, Henry Allison, and Peter Heath. Cambridge: Cambridge University Press, 2002.*

R   *Reflexionen* (1753-1804). *Reflections.* In *Notes and Fragments.* Edited by Paul Guyer. Translated by Curtis Bowman, Paul Guyer, and Frederick Rauscher. Cambridge: Cambridge University Press, 2005.* 17: 229–19: 654.

Rel   *Die Religion innerhalb der Grenzen der Bloßen Vernunft* (1794). *Religion within the Boundaries of Mere Reason.* In *Religion and Rational Theology.* Translated and edited by Allen W. Wood and George di Giovanni. Cambridge: Cambridge University Press, 1996.* 6: 3-202.

TP   *Über der Gemeinspruch. Das mag in der Theorie Richtig sein, stimmt aber nicht für die Praxis* (1793). *On the Common Saying: That May Be Correct in Theory, but It Is of No Use in Practice.* In *Practical Philosophy.* Translated and edited by Mary J. Gregor. Cambridge: Cambridge University Press, 2008.* 8: 275-312.

UNH   *Allgemeine Naturalgeschichte und Theorie des Himmels* (1755). *Universal Natural History and Theory of the Heavens.* Edited by Milton K. Munitz. Translated by W. Hastie. Ann Arbor: University of Michigan Press, 1969. 1: 215-368.

WRP   *Welches sind die wirklichen Fortschritte, die Metaphysik seit Leibnitzens und Wolf's Zeiten in Deutschland gemacht hat?* (1793/1804). *What Real Progress Has Metaphysics Made in Germany since the Time of Leibniz and Wolff?* In *Theoretical Philosophy after 1781.* Translated by Henry Allison, Peter Heath, Gary Hatfield, and Michael Friedman. Edited by Henry Allison and Peter Heath. Cambridge: Cambridge University Press, 2002.*

CHAPTER ONE

Introduction

This book is written for people who have an interest in theology and who have encountered the figure of Immanuel Kant, and who want to know more about his thought and significance.

It is difficult to know more about Immanuel Kant, for a number of reasons. His texts are difficult. Reading Kant can be initially confusing and demoralizing rather than illuminating. This problem is compounded by the fact that Kant's thought is a system with many facets. Simply reading one text in isolation can lead to a distorted impression of what is going on, even in that text itself. The literature on Kant is also difficult, as well as being vast, and rapidly expanding, with seemingly irreconcilable fundamental perspectives on Kant's intentions, significance, and meaning. Excellent introductions to Kant's general philosophy do exist.[1] There are also commendable introductions to Kant's philosophy of religion.[2] But these treatments do not have as a central focus Kant's lifelong concern with God, freedom, and happiness, from his earliest thought to his dying days. These themes are likely to be of the greatest interest to the theologically engaged. Furthermore, I relate these topics to Kant's theory of knowledge, and to his shifting views about what metaphysics can achieve. In the course of doing this, I draw deeply, but with a light touch, upon a new wave of

---

1. These include, for example, Andrew Ward, *Kant: The Three Critiques* (London: Polity, 2006); Allen W. Wood, *Kant* (Oxford: Wiley-Blackwell, 2004); and Roger Scruton, *Kant,* Past Masters (Oxford: Oxford University Press, 1983), followed by his *Kant: A Very Short Introduction* (Oxford: Oxford University Press, 1993; revised 2001).

2. Lawrence R. Pasternack, *Kant on Religion within the Boundaries of Mere Reason* (Oxford and New York: Routledge, 2014); Pamela Sue Anderson and Jordan Bell, *Kant and Theology* (London and New York: T&T Clark, 2010).

more historically sensitive, theologically open-minded, and holistic Kant interpretation, to which I have contributed.[3] These new developments in Kant scholarship have identified much more continuity between his earlier theological and metaphysical thought, and his later "critical" philosophy. Kant's mature philosophy has standardly been received by theologians as attempting a straightforward refutation of the possibility of theological discourse.[4] The picture of Kant emerging from recent scholarship is quite different, and much more textured about how Kant might relate to theology.

From years of teaching Kant to students whose main interest in Kant is theological, I am convinced that there is no single book available that really brings out what might be of central interest to students of theology, who do not have the time or inclination to dedicate years of their lives to the specialist and technical study of Kant and the secondary literature. By "student of theology" I mean someone who engages thoughtfully with the intellectual tradition, whether that be through a formal course of study or not. My hope is that students of theology will be delighted, surprised, and challenged by what they can learn from an engagement with Kant. Some of these lessons are more positive, with Kant remembering deep strands of the tradition, and applying them in the context of the rise of modern science. Other lessons are more negative, showing where some of the deep fault lines in modern thought really lie. These fault lines are not where one might initially have thought.

This book began its life as a series of public addresses, given as the 2013 McDonald Lectures in Theology, Ethics & Public Life at the University of Oxford. I have extensively reworked the lectures for publication as a book, making the text more appropriate for a different genre, and responding to feedback. Two important features of the lectures, though, I have retained. First of all, I do not presuppose any prior study of philosophy, or of Kant.

3. See Christopher J. Insole, *Kant and the Creation of Freedom* (Oxford: Oxford University Press, 2013); "A Thomistic Reading of Kant's *Groundwork of the Metaphysics of Morals:* Searching for the Unconditioned," *Modern Theology* 31.2 (2015): 284-311; "Kant's Transcendental Idealism and Newton's Divine *Sensorium,*" *Journal of the History of Ideas* 72.3 (2011): 413-36; "Intellectualism, Relational Properties and the Divine Mind in Kant's Pre-Critical Philosophy," *Kantian Review* 16.3 (2011): 399-428; "Kant's Transcendental Idealism, Freedom and the Divine Mind," *Modern Theology* 27.4 (2011): 608-38 (esp. pp. 628-32); "A Metaphysical Kant: A Theological *Lingua Franca?*" *Studies in Christian Ethics* 25.2 (May 2012): 206-14; and "The Irreducible Importance of Religious Hope in Kant's Conception of the Highest Good," *Philosophy* 83.3 (2008): 333-51.

4. See, for example, Nicholas Wolterstorff, "Is It Possible and Desirable for Theologians to Recover from Kant?" *Modern Theology* 14.1 (1998): 1-18.

This is not to say that the text will be easy reading for those with no philosophical or Kantian background. But I do believe it will be possible and rewarding reading, with enough repeated and clear explanations, alongside a glossary of terms, and the use of vivid images and analogies. Second, I have retained several literary devices. These literary devices come in two forms. First of all, there is my use of the notion of conceptual rooms in chapters two and three, where Kant's background assumptions are visualized in terms of architecture, ornamentation, and artifacts. Second, chapters four to eight dramatize the unfolding of Kant's philosophical and theological understanding in terms of Dante's imagined journey, in the *Divine Comedy,* up the mountain of purgatory.

The book is ambitious in its scope and depth, tracking central features of Kant's whole intellectual journey with respect to God, knowledge, freedom, causation, belief, and happiness. It does this by relating Kant to a range of debates and influences. Such ambition, I found, is assisted by imagery and metaphor. For example, by picturing a conceptual room, I am able to depict and specify complex, filigreed, and nuanced degrees and aspects of influence, in a way that would have taken many more thousands of words, qualifications, and hesitations: Newton can be invited into the room as a guest; statues of Plato and Aquinas can be present, but not overbearingly or anachronistically celebrated; people can be present in the room, but without their thought being exhaustively captured by every intellectual commitment that the room is intended to communicate. To take another example, I describe an imagined campfire in chapter four. This image makes it possible to picture historical thinkers sitting close to, or farther away from, a circle of committed followers, nodding at some things, but demurring from others. In ordinary descriptive prose, this would entail an unmemorable business of categorizing positions, without the necessary context to make it appropriately fascinating. But enough content can be conveyed, for our purposes, through the more palatable medium of a visualized scene. In this way, complex arguments and lines of intellectual development can be conveyed in a way that is vivid, memorable, and relatively accessible to those without specialist training, and without writing a book that is twice as long and difficult.

Phases in Kant's intellectual development are related by imagining steps up the mountain of purgatory, where key influences at each stage of Kant's thought are depicted by a cast of influential thinkers and provocations. The imagery of steps, I have found, avoids unhelpful reification or multiplication of "phases" of Kant's thought, easily combining different strands of continuity, gradual development, and rupture, especially as I exploit the idea of a spiral, rather than a linear, ascent. In my choice of a journey metaphor running throughout the book, there is a mirroring of form and content. The narrative content of the book circles around the pressures, opportunities, eclipses, and shifts that occur across an intellectual lifetime. The literary form of a journey is intended to carry such material limpidly and gracefully. Kant's thought unfurls across a developmental temporal arc, with deep spiritual convictions and intellectual treasures tested through crises and resolutions.

Claims that I make throughout are defended with reference to primary texts, and with some reference to my position in relation to the secondary literature. It would not be appropriate in this type of book to engage in extensive wrangling in the field of Kant studies, but nonetheless, I take care when setting out a controversial interpretation of Kant to announce this, and to explain why I think other interpretations are wrong, but also how they have come about, and how some of them have become mainstream. In the chapters themselves, I only include explicit discussion of the secondary literature where I am making a significant and controversial move. The reader needs to be so apprised in order to emerge from the book having learned not only how I interpret Kant, but also something reliable about the current state of Kant studies on key topics of relevance to theologians. More detailed suggestions for further reading, in relation to each chapter, are included at the back of the book.

In the next chapter I begin the substantive treatment of Kant, and set out a map for the argument of the book. In this introduction, I want to summarize not specific claims made by Kant, but dimensions to Kant's thinking that might amaze, delight, illuminate, and even shock the student of theology, when reflecting on the drama of Kant's engagement with the themes of God, freedom, and happiness. There are five strands that emerge at numerous points in the book. At times, I will draw attention to the strands, but more often, their presence will be easily felt without my drawing explicit attention to them.

(1) The tradition of philosophical theology that Kant was immersed in is known as "theological rationalism," and was the dominant intellectual paradigm for thinking theologically in eighteenth-century Germany, and thus for German Enlightenment thought. This school is now deeply unfashionable, and is barely understood or studied at all by non-specialists. Where it is treated, it is presented as a rather arid

reduction of religion to a set of formulas and principles. By engaging with Kant's early and mature philosophy, I hope to show that whatever one thinks of it, there is a theological integrity, energy, beauty, and sincerity to theological rationalism, which has genuine and profound strains from medieval and classical theology. There is even what we might call a living and lived spirituality to it. If this is true, we should find out about it, as it restores to us a forgotten theological texture and dimension to much philosophy from the German Enlightenment.

(2) As well as being immersed in a tradition of philosophical theology, Kant's conception of philosophy itself is rooted in a classical tradition, where philosophy is ordered not only toward the true, but also to the good, and so toward a capacious understanding of human happiness. This puts us in contact with a now largely forgotten tradition of philosophy, of under-appreciated significance to Kant and the Enlightenment. Philosophy is conceived of, in this tradition, as a transformative way of life, which speaks sincerely, longingly even, about God and divinity, albeit eschewing the category of revelation, and, accordingly, harboring doubts about traditional Christian doctrines.

(3) Kant is acutely sensitive to different ways in which we can assent to propositions. Kant is concerned with a range of textures in our (as he puts it) "holding-for-true." Knowledge is only one way in which we "hold for true," and not even the most important way. There are other textures of belief and assent, some arising from our aspirations as finite creatures seeking transcendence. The activity of holding-for-true can be ordered not only to the true, but also to the good, without this making our beliefs fictional or insincere. Arising from Kant's sensitivity to different textures of belief is his interest in the systematicity, unity, and harmony of philosophy. Kant's "system" is not a dry and abstract construction responding to the abstract demands of a method. Rather, it is intended as an orientation toward a cosmos that is itself true, good, and beautiful.

(4) There is something moving about the honesty of Kant's thought, an "ethic" of how and what to believe. Kant pushes constantly against his own system. He refuses to avoid painful intellectual difficulties, as well as refusing to neglect our highest aspirations.

(5) When all is said and done, we struggle to call Kant a Christian. This is not because he does not believe in God. Kant does believe in God, and his conception of God is recognizably indebted to a Christian tradition of reflection on the unconditioned. Rather, the single most

astounding and disruptive challenge of Kant's thought and legacy is in the area of how he thinks about human freedom in relation to God. The biggest challenge to traditional Christianity presented by Kant is intra-doctrinal, and related to how we conceive of human freedom in relation to divine action. By studying Kant, we can understand how an intellectual revolution has occurred in our thinking about freedom, a revolution that is so successful that we are hardly aware that we are its children.

The book is studiedly focused on Kant's thought about God, freedom, and happiness, in relation to the tradition of Christian theology that this aspect of his thought grew out of. The priority given to this aspect of his thought is not to be mistaken with the claim that this is the only, or even the most important, aspect of Kant's thought, for Kant or for his legacy. Kant was concerned with many matters, among which God, freedom, and happiness are undoubtedly important, but not exclusively so. Nonetheless, these themes, above all others, as handled by Kant, will be of central importance to the theologically engaged reader, and therefore to the intended readership of this book.

CHAPTER TWO

"*I Am from Eternity to Eternity*": God in Kant's Early Thought

In the mid-1780s Kant tells us that the concept of God "is the true abyss for human reason":

> One can neither resist nor tolerate the thought of a being represented as the highest of all possible things, which may say to itself, "I am from eternity to eternity, and outside me there is nothing except what exists through my will." (*LPR,* 28: 1033)

At the heart of this book is an extended meditation on what it might mean for us that Kant, a thinker in the bones of modernity, could utter such extraordinary words, that we can neither "resist nor tolerate" the thought of God.

The drama of Kant's lifelong engagement with the themes of God, freedom, and happiness can be encapsulated in a few questions. What is it that we protect when we say that we are "free"? A common instinct and answer is that this involves being ultimately responsible for our actions, and being able to do otherwise than we do. Even if I exercise my freedom by a life of dissolute indulgence and malice, I am still free, even if I might not be happy, and even if I fail to make others happy and fulfilled. We can then go on to ask: is there something more valuable than freedom, even if freedom is part of how we achieve this more valuable goal? A mainstream in Western philosophy has thought that there is: it is achieving our purpose, becoming what we ought to be, flourishing in our properly ordered human nature, which leads to harmony, community, and happiness. This is what Kant tracks with his concept of "the highest good," the *summum bonum.* Here is a central tension in Kant's thought that is traced in this book. We need God, if we are to attain the highest good. We also (perhaps regrettably) need freedom, in order to access the highest good. God must withdraw for freedom to be possible; but as God withdraws, it becomes harder to understand how the highest good will be attained. I have been careful to call this a "tension" and not a "contradiction." Kant, as we will see in chapter eight, achieves a sort of resolution, consistent in its own terms.[1] As we will also see, in so doing, Kant moves away from traditional Christianity. The Christian theologian will always want to talk about God acting upon, and within, us to bring about our transformation, in a way that nonetheless does not destroy our freedom. Kant will not be able to say this.

This chapter sets out the intellectual background for Kant's belief in God, and the shape of Kant's early philosophical theology. The next chapter argues that the mature Kant continues to believe in the same God, and explains why, for Kant, God is essential for our achievement of the highest good. Chapter four sets out the shift in Kant's conception of what freedom involves. Kant moves from a position where he is content for God to determine our actions, without this violating our freedom, to a position where he is deeply unhappy with such a metaphysical picture. Kant shifts to a position where he wants to claim for us a radical ability to do other than we do, arising from our being ultimately responsible for our actions, in contrast to God being ultimately responsible. Kant considers such freedom to be both essential and regrettable; we might say that such freedom is "regrettably essential." Kant is well known for thinking that freedom is essential, less well known for thinking that it is regrettable. Nonetheless, I will argue, this sense of regret is an irreducible feature of Kant's thought. God, for example, is perfectly free, enjoying the highest and paradigmatic expression of freedom. But God cannot do otherwise than the good, and this is an expression of God's true freedom, not a derogation of it.

Kant struggles to find a way to reconcile his new demands on freedom with his underlying metaphysics and theology. In the 1770s Kant calls the problem of how a being "derived from another" can be free "the only un-

---

1. For an alternative account of how Kant resolves this tension, see Lawrence R. Pasternack, *Kant on Religion within the Boundaries of Mere Reason* (Oxford and New York: Routledge, 2014). For my discussion of Pasternack's account see "Christopher Insole on Lawrence Pasternack's 'Kant on Religion,'" https://virtualcritique.wordpress.com/2015/07/01/insole-on-pasternacks-kant-on-religion/. For further discussion, see also Lawrence Pasternack's "Reply to Christopher Insole," https://virtualcritique.wordpress.com/2015/07/01/reply-to-christopher-insole/.

solvable metaphysical problem." He does, though, achieve a resolution to the problem of our being free, given that we are created by God. The shape of this solution is outlined in chapters five and six. Nonetheless, Kant's solution has important and fraught implications for how he thinks of our freedom, and the highest good, in relation to divine action: this is the topic of chapters seven and eight. Kant preserves our freedom in a way that would not be acceptable to the Christian tradition, by pushing back the scope of divine action, to the point where he will even deny that God is the creator of space and time. By the final chapter, we see Kant's system pull itself apart on the question of God and human freedom, fully demonstrating how the concept of God is both intolerable and irresistible.

Curiously, perhaps, Kant does achieve a sort of final peace. In fragmentary writings from his final years, between 1800 and 1803, Kant repeatedly asks, "but is there a God?," "is God real?," "where is God?" And repeatedly his answer is, "in us," "in our moral law giving," "in our reason," "in our rational will," and not "out there." In this chapter and the next, I will argue that this is not Kant's position throughout almost all of his life, from 1750 until the 1790s. But it seems to be his dying thought — which you can express either by saying that there is no God, or that we become as God. There is here a sort of theosis, a becoming divine, albeit that the source and end of this theosis is not, as it would be in the tradition, a transcendent (and immanent) God. Now we do not struggle with an external creator. The non-rigorous but suggestive hope that we have lies in us, where we are our own divine guarantors of both freedom and autonomy.

This suspicion of a late decline in Kant's religious beliefs, or at least in their traditional form, receives some biographical support. A friend of Kant in old age, Karl Ludwig Pörschke, reported of Kant that "he often assured me even when he had been *Magister* for a long time, he did not doubt any dogma *(Satz)* of Christianity. Little by little, one after the other, they broke off."[2] Upon watching Kant's coffin lowered into the earth, another friend, Johann Georg Scheffner, reflects, "you will not believe the kind of tremor that shook my existence when the first frozen clumps of earth were thrown on his coffin — my head and heart still tremble."[3] According to a

2. Manfred Kuehn, *Kant: A Biography* (Cambridge: Cambridge University Press, 2001), p. 138; the citation is from Johann Friedrich Abegg, *Reisetagebuch von 1798* (Frankfurt: Insel Verlag, 1976), p. 184.

3. Kuehn, *Kant: A Biography*, p. 2; citing Scheffner to Lüdeck, March 5, 1804, in *Briefe von und an Scheffner*, 5 vols., ed. Arthur Warda and Carl Driesche (Munich and Leipzig: Duncker and Humblot, 1916), 2: 443.

recent biographer of Kant, Scheffner's unease owed much to his awareness that although in Kant's philosophy "he had held out for eternal life and a future state," in his personal life he had become "cold to such ideas."[4]

Our task now is to understand how we have arrived at this final scene, and to interrogate our reaction to it. Our guiding question is not simply "what did Kant think?" We must also ask, "what is the relationship between freedom and the highest good, and the happiness that is consequent upon this good?" and "how can we be free and happy with or without God?" We will engage these questions, though, by walking side by side with Kant. For reasons explored in the introduction, from chapter four onward, I conceive of Kant's development through the device of imagining Kant as a Virgil-type figure, leading us up the mountain of a Dante-inspired purgatory.

The headline claim for the book will be this: that Kant's conception of both freedom and the highest good would have to be considered religious, but is with difficulty considered fully Christian. Kant's ethic will be revealed as "religious," in that Kant can only understand concepts such as freedom and the highest good by reference to irreducibly theological categories such as an uncreated God, who is the All-of-Reality (which will be explained), the highest good (beyond any partial and experiential good), and created (non-spatial and non-temporal) souls. Kant's ethic can only tendentiously be called "Christian," in that he denies, neglects, or does not know about (a different verb applies to different doctrines) core claims and dimensions of the Christian tradition: for example, incarnation, trinity, divine simplicity, and the concursus between divine action and human freedom (I will explain the notion of concursus in chapter seven). In this space between Kant's religious ethic and a Christian ethic, theologians are entitled to engage with Kant on immanently theological terms, without translating their claims into an acceptably secular significance, or needing to build up to theological presuppositions from ground zero. I propose, in this book, to attempt the experiment of extending to Kant the courtesy of heuristically expanding the distance between his "religious" ethic and a "Christian" ethic, so that we can see in better relief the religious ethic with its own integrity, nuances, strangeness, aspirations, and anxieties. I will allow his religious ethic to be a rich and textured worldview (a spirituality even) with which I am in conversation.

From this perspective, Virgil is not an entirely inapposite compar-

---

4. Kuehn, *Kant: A Biography,* p. 3.

ison. Virgil sees, Dante tells us, "as reason sees," and departs before the reason-transcending mysteries of Christian faith are visible. Similarly, I will suggest, Kant "sees as reason sees," and leaves the Christian theologian before she contemplates some of the reason-transcending mysteries of faith. Virgil's leaving is not a joyous event for Dante:

> He had taken his light from us. He had gone.
> Virgil had gone. Virgil the gentle Father
> to whom I gave my soul for its salvation!
>
> Not all that sight of Eden lost to view
> by our First Mother could hold back the tears
> that stained my cheeks so lately washed with dew.
>
> "Dante, do not weep yet, though Virgil goes.
> Do not weep yet, for soon another wound
> shall make you weep far hotter tears than those!"
>
> (*Purgatorio,* Canto XXX, lines 49-57)

Perhaps, at this stage, and even more so after reading this book, you might find Kant's leaving a sweeter sorrow. Nonetheless, I hope to communicate something of Kant's searing intellectual humility and honesty. He shows us not only a "problem" but the "problem of the problem," and is good to think alongside, even if a parting of the ways becomes inevitable. Before we immerse ourselves in Kant's struggle with God, we will need to understand what Kant understands by the concept of God, both in his early work (the subject of the rest of this chapter), and in his later thought (the topic of the next chapter). Understanding the lines of continuity and discontinuity between the early and late Kant will be vital.

In 1763, Kant writes that "if it be permitted to translate the communings of the Infinite with Himself into human language, we may imagine God addressing himself in these terms":

> *I am from eternity to eternity: apart from me there is nothing, except it be through me.* (*OPA,* 2: 151)

More than twenty years later, in the mid-1780s, Kant repeats a similar line. He evokes a "being represented as the highest of all possible things," who "may say to itself":

I am from eternity to eternity, and outside me there is nothing except what exists through my will; *but whence then am I?* (*LPR,* 28: 1033)

There is repetition here, the being ("the Infinite," the "highest of all possible things") who utters to himself, "I am from eternity to eternity," and "outside me there is nothing except what exists through my will." But in the mid-1780s there is a striking addition: "but whence then am I?"

If we can understand the proper relationship between these two ventriloquized divine utterances, and the significance of the added note of existential self-interrogation in the later passage ("but whence then am I?"), we will be well on the way toward understanding the continuities and shifts in Kant's conception of God.

There is a well-known narrative about the development of Kant's philosophy: that in his early thought, Kant believes in God, and in other traditional metaphysical concepts (for example, the soul, and the principle of sufficient reason), but that his "critical turn" (from 1770 onward) leads Kant to reject such traditional beliefs. The meaning of Kant's "critical turn" will occupy us particularly in chapters four to six; but all are agreed that in some sense, from 1770 onward, Kant intends to tighten up on irresponsible knowledge claims. According to this narrative, the concept of God continues to play a useful "heuristic" role in Kant's mature thought: we act, or think, *as if* there is a God, to engage in particular projects. But now Kant believes not so much in God, but rather believes in the value of the *idea* of God: and even that, perhaps, is mistrusted by commentators as a dying remnant, something that Kant should have, but could not quite, discard. The answer to the question "whence then am I?," on this account, is readily forthcoming: in the mind of rational agents (and nowhere else), as a (more-or-less) useful concept, for specific purposes. Where the theologian might be inclined to complain that a concept that is not held to be true can hardly be very useful, the secular commentator on Kant can be happy to agree, and between the two of them, God is finally removed from Kant's philosophy.

This chapter and the next will offer a different reading of the relationship between the two claims, in the context of an overarching account of Kant's belief in God, from his earliest thought to his very last years. The headline claim of the book will be this: that Kant believes (that is, *really believes*) in the same God in 1763 and in 1785, and through the 1790s. In the first part of the chapter I will show that the concept of God that Kant believes in is saturated in the categories of theological rationalism (a term

I will explain). There is indeed a shift in Kant's later thought about God, tracked here by the question "whence then am I?" This shift is to be located in the way in which Kant thinks we can come to have warranted belief in God, rather than being a shift in what it is that we believe in. This will be the focus of the next chapter. That Kant believes in (the same) God throughout almost all of his life will be the central claim, albeit that the grounds for belief change. Even the final shift away from belief in a divine being who is independent of our minds, I will suggest, is less a transition from religious to secular thinking, and more from one type of religious thinking to another.

Kant's Theological Rationalism in the Pre-Critical Period

If Kant is to be our journeyman and guide in thinking about the relationship between freedom, the highest good, and God, we will want first of all to know something about how Kant thinks, his formation and his background. As well as a journey into the realm of concepts, we might undertake an interior exploration of the foundations of Kant's thinking about God. In his poem "The Old Fools," Philip Larkin talks about the "lighted rooms inside your head," as a metaphor for the memories and experiences that constitute identity. Sometimes in these rooms we find people performing a familiar action, extracting a favorite book from the shelf. Sometimes there is just furniture, a fire, and sunlight. In the rest of this chapter, and in the next chapter, we will step through some of Kant's lighted rooms, where I construe the space in the rooms in conceptual rather than physical terms. We will explore three conceptual spaces: first of all, and only briefly, a room with memories of Kant's Pietist upbringing; second, an impressive rationalist stateroom where Kant spends much of his so-called "early thought"; and finally, in the next chapter, a space that will turn out to be the same room, but some twenty years later.

The first room is orderly, respectable, humble enough. It is the home of a saddle-maker's family. The sage of Königsberg, and the light of Europe, is being dandled on his mother's knee. This is Kant's faithfully Lutheran Pietist childhood home. The movement known as Pietism emphasized the value of personal devotion, which could be manifested by powerful emotive states and by practical ethical actions. Given Kant's subsequent emphasis upon the ethical importance of religion, it is understandable that work has been done drawing out Pietist influences upon Kant. But Kant himself was unfailingly rude about Pietism in later life. He complained that the Pietist was identifiable as the person who "tastelessly makes the idea of religion dominant in all conversation and discourse."[5] Kant was pathologically suspicious of the Pietists' emphasis on emotion and enthusiasm, expressing contempt for their public and collective confessions of faith. Consistent with this attitude, Kant did not go to church in later life and found excuses to avoid University ceremonies at the cathedral in Königsberg. About the religious instruction that he had received at the Pietist *Collegium,* Kant complained that "we need to be sent back to school once again" to understand these doctrines, "if only we could find someone there (besides ourselves) who understood them better."[6]

That said, Kant expressed affection for, and gratitude to, his (Pietist) mother, for "planting in me the seed of morality." And more widely, the debt to strands of Lutheran piety can be detected in later works such as *Religion within the Boundaries of Mere Reason* and in Kant's later emphasis upon morality as the route to religious belief. Nonetheless, the textual evidence from the 1750s onward suggests that the dominant theological influence on Kant is not Lutheranism, but a theological rationalism informed by medieval theology, with strands of influence from Plato and Aristotle that would hardly have found favor with Luther himself. When, in *Religion within the Boundaries of Mere Reason,* Kant sets out to translate an admittedly very Lutheran religious vocabulary into the terms of "mere reason," the "reason" is not so much secular ethics as Kant's version of theological rationalism. I will justify this claim in the next chapter, but at this point we need to define the tradition and spirituality in question. What is "theological rationalism" and how does it express itself in Kant's thought? To find out, we need to enter the second room.

Even if it is not to our taste, this next space is impressive. A lofty room in an eighteenth-century palace, classical in structure and proportion, but with rich ornamentation. Tapestries of diverse natural subjects hang on the walls, forming harmonious, beautiful, and ordered patterns. In this room Leibniz is talking loudly, as are the more obscure figures of Christian Wolff and Alexander Baumgarten. Baumgarten is the author of metaphysical textbooks that Kant lectured from throughout his whole life. Plato and Aquinas are not there in person, although there are busts of them;

5. Allen W. Wood, "Kant's Life and Works," in *A Companion to Kant,* ed. Graham Bird (Oxford: Wiley-Blackwell, 2010), pp. 10-31 (p. 11).

6. Wood, "Kant's Life and Works," p. 11.

and Leibniz has engaged with them directly and extensively. With a jolt of surprise, we see Isaac Newton in the corner, although he has been invited by some of the members. These same members are highly animated, and seem very eager to have Newton on their side; Newton does not seem similarly animated, but nor does he look uncomfortable. In the circle around Newton is Martin Knutzen, a vital influence on Kant's early intellectual development as a student.

If we were to eavesdrop for a while, we would get a sense of some important preoccupations of the eighteenth-century rationalist. At least three questions emerge:

(1) What are the limits upon what is really possible?
(2) What makes possible any particular possibility, and the whole sum total of all possibilities? Upon what do they depend?
(3) How do these possibilities relate to the outstanding success of Newtonian accounts of the physical universe? (Newton himself is keeping quiet about this, but others are answering for him.)

The third question does not concern us now, but will become relevant in the fourth and fifth chapters. Let us listen to the answers that emerge, and those that are rejected, to the first two questions.

Consider the first question: "what are the limits upon the really possible?" It quickly becomes clear that a certain sort of answer is not very popular — the answer that asserts that anything is possible if it is logically possible, that is to say, if it does not involve a self-contradiction of the form *"a and not-a":* "the bachelor is married" is still a favorite example in the philosophical literature, where "bachelor" means unmarried man. You can see that there could not be an unmarried married man. David Hume would be associated with this minimalist account of the limits to possibility. In as much as Hume would think he had to answer the question of what the limits are upon the really possible, he would give this answer: anything is possible that does not generate a self-contradiction. This generates more surprising results than one might think. All sorts of things are "logically" possible that seem quite extraordinary and beyond belief: "the moon is conscious"; "the sun is made of cheese"; "the blowfish can turn itself into water." None of these statements obviously generate a logical contradiction, although they are wildly implausible. But if our only restraint upon possibility is logical, they are indeed possibilities.

Now I am about to subject you to a few paragraphs where I raise the important question of "whether or not salt necessarily dissolves in water." The question is not whether or not it does (even philosophers know that it does), but whether in some sense it *has* to, if it is to remain salt. I promise that there will be important, even dramatic, theological implications in either case. This matters, as everyone in the rationalist room believes in God, or claims to. So, is it the case that "salt necessarily dissolves in water"? That is to say, could something be salt, and yet not dissolve in water, when water is in a liquid state, and all the other conditions are correct for salt dissolving? Could we imagine a parallel universe, where something has all the properties of salt, and meets something with all the properties of water, and yet where salt does not dissolve in water, just because it does not? In such a world the "laws of nature" are radically different, even though salt is sodium chloride, and water is H_2O. According to the Humean picture, although, for example, fire has certain properties and will behave in certain ways when other things happen (setting fire to things and being hot), and although salt dissolves in water in a liquid state, it is really possible that properties could be differently combined: that H_2O does not behave like water, and that salt does not dissolve in water, and that fire does not set fire to things, or give off heat.

We might not care much about salt, but when we roll out the same question with respect to other matters, things quickly become electric. What about human beings? Are there ways in which human beings always do, or always should behave in interaction with other realities? Or could one be a human being and behave in radically different ways? There are also implications for how we think about God. If anything is possible that is logically possible, and if God can do anything that is possible, then it is up to God to choose which logical possibilities are made real. It will also be up to God to choose whether or not to continue sustaining the same combinations of possibilities. God is busy willing and choosing things. There is a potential for God to be a "busy-body," intervening and changing the course of nature as the divine will pleases. Some have detected such a God in the work of Isaac Newton, and found in it an intriguing source of the observational method. We need to keep looking at nature, to check that God has not changed his mind about how to combine things.

Much more acceptable to most of the people in the rationalist room is an account of the "really possible" along the following lines. The way in which things can be is structured by constraints that go beyond the demand that things not be logically self-contradictory. Some properties will always attach to particular types of substance, where "substance" means here finite entities capable of having properties. These properties will always be combined in a (finite) number of ways. Substances with particular sets of properties will always react to particular events, and interact with other substances in particular ways. So, for example, sodium chloride will always dissolve in water under certain circumstances. These constraining structures have been called variously the "forms" or "essences" that constitute reality: on this account, human nature has an essence (the "what it is to be human"), as do other natural kinds (such as water and salt). Kant believes, for example, that salt will always dissolve in water (and that even God could not stop this). Marvel at, and pity, the wretched sinning salt molecule that could elect not to dissolve in water. Well, *ecce homo;* this is the human being we will meet in future chapters (especially in chapter eight).

If the more minimalist account of possibility as merely logical possibility gives rise to an interventionist and busy God, does this richer account of "real possibility" give rise to a more *laissez-faire* God, who just lets things unfold according to their proper nature? It is easy to get the sense that theological rationalism supports the notion of a semi-independent realm of structured possibilities and natural laws. Theological rationalism can then seem to tip over into deism, the view that God creates the world in its initial state, but then permits the ordered world to run like clockwork, without constantly sustaining it in existence. If theological rationalism does tip over into deism, then any lived sense of divine intimacy and activity is damaged, with an abstract notion of reason substituting for God.

Such a picture would be unfair to the theological rationalist, and misses the main driving force of the theological vision, which is to insist that there is more to the being of God than an arbitrary will. In the rationalist theological conception everything constantly depends, both for its essence (its "what-it-is-ness") and its existence ("whether it is"), on the plenitudinous action of divine self-outpouring. God is acting, or be-ing (as an active verb), everywhere, such that if God were to cease be-ing, everything and every possibility would simply and entirely cease. By its own lights, at least, theological rationalism does endorse the depth and totality of dependence of all things on God. Reason is not independent of God, but identical with God, a part of God, which elevates reason to a cosmic and theological level, as much as it reduces God to a formula. Reason might be "independent" of the divine will, but to say this is simply to say that God can only be God, and that God cannot will not to be God. Whatever one thinks of theological rationalism, one should understand its deepest spiritual wellspring, even if then to reject it. Theological rationalism is as much about the theology as the rationalism, in that everything rational is understood through its being a part of the very uncreated being of God. If we fail to try to see this, we will be blind to one of the great spiritual aspirations of a strand of Enlightenment philosophy.

On neither the interventionist nor the rationalist account, you might think, is there much space for a standard modern notion of freedom, where we can do other than we do, and where we are ultimately responsible for our actions? The interventionist God can constantly interfere with our projects, and perhaps with our freedom itself. The situation looks even worse on the rationalist conception, where everything unfolds according to an essence sustained in, and activated by, the divine nature. We should reflect here on the following thought, to be fully explored in later chapters: in the premodern Christian philosophical tradition, our being free is entirely compatible with God acting in our every action, everywhere and all the time. In fact, this is the only thing that freedom truly is. It will be this conception that Kant begins to react against in the 1760s and 1770s.

It is not enough to be classed as a theological rationalist simply to believe in "essences" or "forms." Aristotelians also believe in essences, as indeed do a recent wave of analytical philosophers known as the "new essentialists," who argue that the practice of science needs some sort of commitment to essences.

Theological rationalists are also very interested in the answer to our second question: "What makes possible any particular possibility, and the whole sum total of all possibilities? Upon what do they depend?" We do not hear any rationalists in the room saying that each particular possibility and the "sum total of all possibilities" are just brute: "this is just what they are." Rather, the only thing that grounds possibilities is that they participate in a greater reality, a dynamic, emanating, self-giving plenitude of actuality. The lesser comes from the greater. This is a principle that can find no resting point until we come to a fullness of plenitude and perfection from which everything derives. Hence, in rationalist accounts, drawing upon a perennial Platonic tradition, there are characteristically strong patterns of desire, of stretching out for completion, fulfillment, and for that which is more perfect.

This is quite a different intuitive paradigm than most contemporary people will have, until and unless they expose themselves to premodern thought. We are more likely to think that the complex arises from the more simple. For example, the paradigm of evolution teaches us that more complex organisms arise from less complex organisms. More complex structures build up from microscopic particles. We go from less to more; but the theological rationalist from the more to the less. What is the plenitudinous resting place and ground for all reality? For the theological rationalist, there must be a deep structure behind all things, of which the world as we know it is a derivative shadow and emanation. This deep structure must be mind, the most perfect dimension of reality; and a theological rationalist will always find that it is mind with both understanding *and will,* because at the heart of all that is, is a free action of creation. This mind that grounds all possibilities is God. To sum up: from our eavesdropping, we have the following outline for eighteenth-century rationalist theology: the divine mind is the source and ground of all real possibilities, where there are essential structures to what is really possible, over and above the logically possible. This is Kant's view.

If we appreciate the theological seriousness of theological rationalism, we will be ready to have our attention drawn to two important implications of the particular way in which Kant appropriates this tradition for his wider thought: the first implication will be that things can depend utterly upon God, without depending at all upon the divine will; the second implication will be that God's perfect freedom does not always involve the divine will being able to do other than it does. To draw out these implications, let us now turn to some passages from Kant, which confirm him as a theological rationalist on the account I have just given, and which enable us to draw out the further implications. These passages are taken from his earlier work (the 1760s), although I will show in the next chapter that he continues to hold this view in his later "critical philosophy."

Before engaging with these difficult passages, I want to set out an image, an analogy, that should assist comprehension. When reading Kant on God, it is helpful to grasp that the God-concept is split into two parts for Kant: the divine understanding and the divine will.[7] Imagine, if you like, that the divine understanding is a sort of rummage box. In this rummage box exist all the "real possibilities," the "essences" from which

---

7. Some theological readers will worry at this point that Kant does not abide by the doctrine of divine simplicity, whereby in God and God alone there is a deep identity between reason, will, divine existence, and all divine properties and action. Such readers would be right. Kant ostensibly endorses divine simplicity, but means by this no more than that God cannot be split by anything external (*OPA,* 2: 84-85; *LPR,* 28: 1038). There is nowhere in Kant's work an explicit understanding of what the classical doctrine of divine simplicity involves.

God can choose. God did not choose how to fill up the rummage box. This is just how it is. The divine will, if you like, "discovers" these possibilities in the divine understanding. The divine will can choose which of the real possibilities to instantiate, by creating them in a world. If Kant was more of a classical Platonist, rather than an eighteenth-century rationalist (with Platonic strands), then we would have to also say that the realities in the rummage box are more perfect archetypal forms of the particular realities that we find in the world, where the latter are a less intense and partial participation in the world of forms: the imperfect human participating in a perfect form of humanity, a partial goodness or beauty participating in a plenitudinous and paradigmatic archetype of goodness and beauty. The realities in Kant's rummage box, though, are fairly hum-drum in themselves, and expressed quite directly in the created world: things like salt, fire, and human beings. The glory of the "rummage-box-plus-will" picture lies elsewhere. First of all, one finds it in the superb order, beauty, and harmony that exist between all the real possibilities in the rummage box. It is the best, fullest, and most harmonious rummage box that there could ever be. The second glory is the wisdom by which God chooses which possibilities to create. Wisdom is an expression of the harmony between God's will and the order and beauty in the rummage box. God is not, and never could be, a bad chooser: he is the best possible chooser, from the best possible rummage box.

All this rummage box talk should cast a flattering light upon Kant's more elevated language:

> All the unity and harmony I observe around me is only possible because a Being exists which contains within it the grounds not only of reality but also of all possibility. (*OPA*, 2: 152-53)

> This Supreme Being embraces within itself everything which can be thought by man, when he, a creature made of dust, dares to cast a spying eye behind the curtain which veils from mortal eyes the mysteries of the inscrutable. God is all-sufficient. Whatever exists, whether it be possible or actual, is only something in so far as it is given through Him. If it be permitted to translate the communings of the Infinite with Himself into human language, we may imagine God addressing Himself in these terms: *I am from eternity to eternity: apart from me there is nothing, except it be through me.* (*OPA*, 2: 151)

Here we have the fuller context for the passage which I began this chapter with. Kant goes onto reflect that

> This thought, of all thoughts the most sublime, is still widely neglected, and mostly not considered at all. That which is to be found in the possibilities of things and which is capable of realizing perfection and beauty in excellent schemes has been regarded as a necessary object of Divine Wisdom but not itself as a consequence of this Incomprehensible Being. The dependency of other things has been limited to their existence alone. As a result of this limitation, a large share in the ground of so much perfection has been taken away from that Supreme Nature, and invested in I know not what absurdity. (*OPA,* 2: 151)

What does Kant mean here, and what precisely has been "neglected"? To help us see this, we need to understand what precisely Kant means by saying that the possibility of all things "depends" upon God. Kant helps us here, by distinguishing between what he calls "moral" and "non-moral" dependency upon God. We have "moral" dependence when God decides, through his will, to create something out of nothing, and to sustain it in existence. This sort of dependence, Kant thinks, is widely known about, and is what he is referring to when he writes about the "dependency of . . . things" inasmuch as we are concerned with "their existence alone." In other words, things depend for their existence upon the divine will, inasmuch as God selects them from the rummage box.

This still misses out "a large share in the ground of so much perfection" that belongs to "the Supreme Nature." To grasp this we need to understand that the structure of *all* possibilities is grounded by God, in that they are the consequences of the divine *understanding,* but not of the divine *will.* This sort of dependence upon God Kant calls "non-moral dependence." This is what it means to say that although God is not constantly intervening, God does not withdraw: it is the "be-ing" of God (think verb) that keeps the whole structure of possibility going. It includes, Kant tells us, *all possibility,* "everything which can be thought by man," "whatever exists, whether it be possible or actual" (*OPA,* 2: 151). It ranges from the most abstract possibility of a geometrical proof, to the concrete atmospheric realities of air and water (*OPA,* 2: 101-3). It also includes all principles of order, harmony, beauty, rationality, and goodness (*OPA,* 2: 91-92; 101-3; 151-54). The divine *"all-sufficiency"* that grounds all possibility is "expanded to include all that is possible or real," and "designates everything which can be conceived under the notion of perfection" (*OPA,* 2: 154).

If you are not used to the idea, it needs a bit of effort to wrap your mind around it, and not to think you have understood it before you really have. It is certainly not the view that God, through his will, "creates" the structure of possibility as such. This prioritizing of the divine will has its proponents in the history of theology, and is known as "voluntarism," from the Latin *voluntas,* meaning "will." Kant is not a voluntarist about possibilities: the structure of real possibilities is given independently of the divine will.[8] But it is not the case that *God* is presented with an external and independent set of possibilities, from which God then chooses. The divine understanding is not something that God finds outside of himself. It is emphatically not this position. Kant (unfairly) ascribes such a view to Leibniz, and then laments, "to what limitations, emanating from a separate ground, would not the Independent Being be subject, if not even these possibilities were grounded in that Being?" (*OPA,* 2: 151). All possibilities are just as dependent upon God, *qua* the divine understanding, as existing realities are dependent upon God, *qua* the divine will. This position is a version of what is known as "intellectualism." According to intellectualism, real possibilities do not exist independently of God, but rather they reside in the divine intellect (what I have been calling the divine "understanding"): hence, "intellectualism" grounds possibilities in the intellect, "voluntarism" in the will.

You could put it like this: what, fundamentally speaking, are possibilities? They are a constituent part of the uncreated divine understanding, and nothing else. God *is,* in part, the rummage box. And without the divine understanding, there simply are no possibilities at all. In this sense, relating to the quotation above, all possibilities are "consequences" (without being created or caused) of the being of the "Incomprehensible Being." God's will, when choosing what to create, is indeed "constrained" (or shaped), but not by something external to God: God's will is constrained fundamentally by God's nature, which in turn is the ground of all possibility. Every law of nature, governing the properties of everything from salt to human beings to planetary motions, is an actualization of a subset of real

8. For a voluntarist reading of Kant's early philosophical theology, see Rae Langton, *Kantian Humility: Our Ignorance of Things in Themselves* (Oxford: Oxford University Press, 2004), chap. 5. For my critique of Langton and voluntarist readings, see Christopher J. Insole, "Intellectualism, Relational Properties and the Divine Mind in Kant's Pre-Critical Philosophy," *Kantian Review* 16.3 (2011): 399-428; and my *Kant and the Creation of Freedom* (Oxford: Oxford University Press, 2013), chap. 3.

possibilities contained in the divine nature. Such order and harmony, and the realization of all real possibilities that are compatible with each other, we might say, are things that all rational wills could universally will. Later on in our journey with Kant, he will say something similar in relation to autonomy, as I will discuss in chapter eight.

So convinced is Kant of this line of thought, from possibility to God, that in his early thought it constitutes a proof, a demonstration, of the necessary existence of God: that anything is possible at all, indicates that there must be God, from which all possibilities come. On this point, there will be an important shift in Kant's later thought. Although I will argue that Kant continues to believe in a rationalist conception of God, he will move away from any confidence that he can prove it, or claim to have knowledge.

Conclusion

We are now ready to draw out the anticipated two implications of Kant's philosophical theology, which will propel us into the following chapters. First of all, the very structure of reason, goodness, harmony, order, and perfection is an aspect of the being of God. But it is not a product of the divine will. This will be of huge significance. Something can depend upon God without being the product of divine will; it depends upon God in the sense that it is an aspect of the uncreated being of God. So the moral law, through which we can become autonomous, might not be commanded by the divine will; it could still, nonetheless, be dependent upon the uncreated being of God, and so be an aspect of divinity.

The second implication I want to draw out from Kant's philosophical theology is this. Divine freedom consists in the divine will choosing in a way that is harmonious with God's self-understanding: the harmony between the will and self-understanding is "wisdom." Because the harmony that constitutes the divine self-understanding is goodness itself ("What is goodness?" "It is an aspect of the being of God"), the divine will always chooses the good: that which is harmonious, universal, and ordered. The divine will is unable to do otherwise, and herein lies its perfect and divine freedom. This strand of Kant's rationalism finds its way into his 1785 work, the *Groundwork of the Metaphysics of Morals,* where Kant sets out his mature understanding of the supreme principle of morality. Here Kant writes that in God "reason infallibly determines the will," where "the will is a capacity to choose *only that* which reason independently of inclination cognizes as . . . good" (*GW,* 4: 412). God's "volition is of itself necessarily in accord with the law" (*GW,* 4: 414), and "his maxims necessarily harmonize with the laws of *autonomy*" (*GW,* 4: 439, emphasis mine).

We will see in chapters four and five how vital it becomes for Kant that human freedom is able to choose between good and evil, if the human being is to be genuinely free. We can only understand the fragility and cutting nuance of this shift in Kant's thought, when we grasp that it is not what Kant thinks *perfect freedom* consists in. Kant's account of human freedom is emphatically and knowingly a description of a structurally imperfect freedom.

In relation to Kant's philosophical theology, you might say: "this is all very well," or, less committedly, "this is as may be," but is this not all from the boring and irrelevant part of Kant's life, before he became philosophically alive (reading Hume and Newton), and critical of traditional theological categories? Is not all this stuff about the divine understanding and divine will just the sort of metaphysical speculation that Kant abandons, when he sets the boundaries of knowledge to that which has some purchase for experience? Well, in short, no, it is not. The next chapter explains and justifies this answer.

CHAPTER THREE

"Whence Then Am I?": God in Kant's Later Thought

In the previous chapter, I offered an exploration of Kant's mindset by passing through two conceptual rooms, depicting crucial parts of his formation in philosophical theology and religiosity: the first was the Pietist space of his childhood and the second a lofty chamber of eighteenth-century theological rationalism. The conception of God we found in Kant's early philosophy was this. The being of God is as much a verb as a noun, giving life to everything that exists. This being is conceived of as composed of a will and an understanding. The divine understanding is made up of all the possible ways in which things can be, or "essences." From this realm of ordered and harmonious possibilities, the divine will chooses to create some things and not others. The divine will can choose whether or not to instantiate an essence, but not what the structure of the essence is. Nonetheless, this structure, and the structure of all perfection, order, and beauty, still depend upon God, in that they depend upon the divine understanding.

At the beginning of this chapter, we find ourselves in another of the "lighted rooms" that constitute Kant's interior reality and formation. This is another impressive eighteenth-century room. At first, it looks different from the previous room: more understated, with less baroque ornamentation. But as our eyes focus, it becomes clear that the view out of the windows is the same, and that it is the same room, except that it is now in the mid-1780s, around twenty years after our first visit. Once we pay attention, we find that the same elaborate detailing is in fact evident, with beautiful, harmonious depictions of the ordered realm of nature, albeit in more subtle and delicate stitching. There are still plenty of books by Leibniz, Wolff, and Baumgarten on the shelves, as well as Newtonian illustrations and demonstrations. In a newly prominent place, pushed against a high sun-comprehending window, are both a microscope and a telescope, pointed at the skies. Also new, since last time, is a miniature of David Hume, prominently placed upon the writing desk, and a portrait of Rousseau over the fireplace. The significance of these additions will occupy us in chapters four and five, as also will the salience of the books hidden under the cushion at the end of the chaise longue, placed there almost so as to hide them. They are works by an eccentric Swedish aristocrat, Baron von Swedenborg, who claims to have contact with spirits of the dead. As with the portraits, the significance of these books by Swedenborg will come to light in chapter five.

But the task for this chapter is different: to justify and understand my claim that Kant, twenty years later, in the height of his mature critical philosophy, is still in the same theologically rationalist space for thinking about God that we found him in twenty years ago. This is of central importance to set up the main drama of this volume: the struggle between freedom and the highest good, and Kant's extraordinary claim that we can neither "resist nor tolerate" the idea of God. We need to know, first of all, whether Kant continues to believe in God at all. After all, if Kant no longer believes in God, then there can hardly be a problem relating a (nonexistent) God to human freedom. Second, we need to know what the God is that Kant believes in, when he encounters his crises in relating freedom and the highest good, and human freedom and divine action.

On the writing desk, we notice a sheet of paper, written in Kant's own hand. It is an extract from the end of the first *Critique,* written in 1781:

> All interest of my reason . . . is united in the following three questions:
> (1.) What can I know?
> (2.) What should I do?
> (3.) What can I hope? (A 805/B 833)

This chapter will set out Kant's answers to each of these questions in turn, with reference to knowledge or belief in God. The headline claims for each part of the chapter will be as follows. First of all, the answer to "what can I know?" will be that we can know what the concept of "God" means, but we cannot know whether or not such a God exists or is real. The answer to "what should I do?" will be that we should be moral. To explain this answer I will introduce a distinction, central to Kant, between reason in its theoretical and practical uses. Briefly, reason is being used theoretically, when answering our first question, "what can I know?"; and reason is being used practically when answering the second question, "what should I do?" In fact, as the third part of the chapter shows, reason (and not wishful thinking) is also being used practically when answering the third question, "What can I hope?" This will be highly significant, because what we can (or even *must*) hope for, Kant thinks, is the God of theological rationalism. So, we cannot know that God exists, but we must be moral, and belief in God is required to support morality.

If we turn over the same piece of paper on Kant's writing desk, we find a few other prominent passages in his own hand, taken from the 1780s, which underline that Kant himself feels questions of God are of enduring significance for his critical philosophy:

> Theology and morality were the two incentives, or better, the points of reference for all the abstract inquiries of reason to which we have always been devoted. (A 853/B 881)

> Thus I had to deny **knowledge** in order to make room for **faith**. (B xxx)

> The entire armament of reason . . . is directed only at the three problems . . . **what is to be done** if the will is free, if there is a God, and *if there is a future world?* (A 800/B 828)

> **God, freedom,** and **immortality of the soul** are those problems at the solution of which all the apparatus of metaphysics aims as its final and sole aim. (*CJ*, 5: 473)

It is worth collecting these passages and dwelling on them a little, to bring to light that Kant's conception of philosophy is in continuity with a classical sense that philosophy should lead us to the good. On such a conception, philosophy is a way of life, ordering us toward happiness and wisdom, more than it is an abstract set of principles or knowledge. We can find other passages, late in Kant's life, where he makes clear his loyalty to such a conception of philosophy, which he tells us is the "doctrine of wisdom" concerned with the "*final end* of human reason," where the "key-stone of the edifice" is "moral practical," and "not just technical-practical" (*OP*, 28: 489).[1] "Wisdom," Kant writes, "is the highest principle of reason"

---

1. For these references in Kant concerning philosophy and wisdom, I am indebted to Pierre Hadot, *What Is Ancient Philosophy?* (Cambridge, MA: Harvard University Press, 2002), pp. 258-70.

(*OP*, 28: 38). "Only the supreme being is wise" (*OP*, 28: 38), Kant writes, so that all that we can possess is the "love of wisdom," as wisdom for us is "transcendent," and philosophy a "progression" (*OP*, 21: 155). Philosophy, as the etymology tells us, is the love of wisdom, but not necessarily, and not for Kant, its possession. Kant gestures approvingly to ancient philosophy, writing that "a hidden idea of philosophy has long been present among men":

> Yet either they have not understood it, or else they have considered it a contribution to erudition. If we take the ancient Greek philosophers — such as Epicurus, Zeno, Socrates — we discover that the principal object of their science has been the destination of man, and the means to achieve it. They thus remained much more faithful to the true Idea of the philosopher than has been the case in modern times, when we encounter the philosopher only as an artist of reason. (*LPE*, 29: 9)

Kant is unambiguous that the "ancient philosophers" are those who approach "the model of the true philosopher." This model Kant does not find represented in "books filled with prescriptions which tell us how we ought to act," but which "show us no means" of attaining the demands laid out in them (*LPE*, 29: 9). Such an "idea of the philosopher" can only be an ideal, as "there exists no philosopher corresponding to this model, any more than there exists any true Christian":

> The "philosopher" is only an idea. Perhaps we may glance at him, and imitate him in some ways, but we shall never totally reach him. (*LPE*, 29: 8)

> There is still a teacher in the ideal. . . . Him alone we must call the philosopher; however . . . he himself is still found nowhere. (A 839/B 867)

In the previous chapter, I suggested that attending to Kant could help to challenge a prejudice against the strand of German Enlightenment thinking known as "theological rationalism." Attending to Kant's own self-conception of his task as a philosopher should, in turn, subvert some easy characterizations of the Enlightenment as leading only to skeptical and abstract patterns of reasoning, uninterested in more capacious conceptions of human flourishing. As Pierre Hadot puts it, we see in this strand of Kant's thought, and throughout his work, a tendency to "force philosophy to leave the closed, fixed circle of the school so that it could become accessible to everyone":

> We must emphasize this characteristic of the philosophy of the eighteenth century, which tends, as in antiquity, to reunite philosophical discourse and way of life.[2]

Or, as Kant puts it:

> Plato asked an old man who told him that he was listening to lectures on virtue: "When are you finally going to start *living* virtuously?" The point is not always to speculate; ultimately, we must think of actual practice. Nowadays, however, he who lives in a way which conforms with what he teaches is taken to be a dreamer. (*LPE*, 29: 12)

Philosophy, for Kant, is a way of life, and concerns the shape of a life ordered toward the ideal of wisdom. This is what it is for philosophy to be "practical." In contrast to the philosopher, as Hadot puts it, "the friend of opinion" does "not see the unity of the universally human interest which animates all philosophical effort."[3] In the second *Critique* Kant even insists that all philosophy is "ultimately practical," and that the interest that attaches to theoretical knowledge "is only conditional and is complete in practical use alone" (*CPrR*, 5: 121). By the end of the chapter, we will understand better how Kant's "devotion" to theology and morality, and his ideal of philosophy as wisdom, work themselves out in his mature thought. Kant claims in his mature thought to "deny knowledge in order to make room for faith." That seems a good place to start. What then, if anything, "can I know" with reference to God?

Theological Rationalism in Kant's Later Thought

In the previous chapter, I set out two almost identical quotations from Kant, one from 1763, the other from 1785. In both quotations, Kant imagines the "communings of the Infinite with Himself." So from 1763:

2. Hadot, *What Is Ancient Philosophy?* p. 268.
3. Hadot, *What Is Ancient Philosophy?* p. 267.

I am from eternity to eternity: apart from me there is nothing, except it be through me. (OPA, 2: 151)

And then from 1785:

I am from eternity to eternity, and outside me there is nothing except what exists through my will; *but whence then am I? (LPR, 28: 1033)*

I claimed that if we could understand the significance of the added note of divine self-interrogation *"but whence then am I?"* we would be well on the way to understanding lines of continuity and discontinuity in Kant's philosophical theology. To get to this point, I first need to show that when talking about God in his later philosophy, Kant continues to mean the God of theological rationalism. We will see, though, that Kant no longer thinks we can know that such a God exists. The movement of thought is this: if there is a God, this is what God would be.

In both the first *Critique* and his *Lectures on the Philosophical Doctrine of Religion,* given in the mid-1780s, Kant returns to his proof from possibility to God, offered in 1763, as discussed in the previous chapter. Kant remains positive about the proof's role in providing the *content* for the concept of God, whatever we might say about the status of the belief in the *existence* of God. In the first *Critique* Kant asks us to hold in mind the concept of the "All of reality," which "contains as it were the entire storehouse of material" from which all possibilities derive. Everything that exists can be understood as a limitation of this total set of all possibilities, whereby some possibilities are made actual, but not others:

All true negations are then nothing but **limits**, which they could not be called unless they were grounded in the unlimited (the All). (A 575/B 603–A 576/B 604)

At the same time, and here is the discontinuity with his earlier thought, Kant is clear that this does not deliver *knowledge* that there is such a being "conforming to the ideal" of the "All of reality." Hence the same space is stripped back, more subtle, understated. Kant tells us that there is "only the idea of such a being" (A 577-78/B 605-6). What we have secured is not the "objective relation of an actual object to other things," but "only that of an **idea**," where we remain in "complete ignorance" about the "existence of a being of such preeminent excellence" (A 579/B 607).

Immediately after saying "whence then am I?" Kant sets out a further thought in relation to the concept of God:

> Here everything falls away beneath us, and the greatest perfection, as much as the smallest, hovers without any support before speculative reason, and it costs reason nothing to let them both disappear, nor is there the least obstacle to this. In short, an absolutely necessary thing will remain to all eternity an insoluble problem for the human under-standing. (*LPR,* 28: 1033)

Kant is "certain" that we can never discover a demonstration sufficient for *theoretical* knowledge claims that "there is a God" and "a future life":

> For whence will reason derive the ground for such experience and their inner possibility? (A 742/B 770)

Theoretical knowledge requires as its source and guarantor reliable experience. For something to be a reliable experience, it must have a spatial and temporal location, and be accessible to all rational people: it must occur in this place, for a certain duration of time, such that all properly rational people would also experience it. The Kant who insists on this discipline about forming beliefs is well known, and has haunted theology for more than two hundred years. Less often appreciated, though, is that this principled impossibility of knowledge about the existence of God cuts two ways, as a *lack* of experience of God does not constitute grounds to doubt the existence of God. So Kant is also "certain" that "no human being" will ever be able to assert that there is no God (A 742/B 770):

> The same grounds for considering human reason incapable of asserting the existence of such a being, when laid before our eyes, also suffice to prove the unsuitability of all counter-assertions. (A 641/B 669)

Nonetheless, if this were the whole story, then we would indeed be inclined to say that Kant no longer believes in God. This conclusion can seem to gather strength when we consider Kant's refutation of traditional proofs for the existence of God in the first *Critique:* for example, Kant denies that we can know that God exists simply by reflecting upon the concept of God, and he denies that the apparent evidence of order and design in the natural world points to a divine designer. At this point we need to reflect upon the significance of Kant's demolition of traditional proofs for the existence of God.

The significance of Kant's refutations of the proofs for the existence of God is set in proper perspective when we realize that he offered more or less identical criticisms of these arguments in 1763, in the undeniable full bloom of his confident knowledge that there is a God as the source of all possibility. Kant has always argued that we cannot know that God exists simply by studying the concept of God. In some of his earliest works, from the mid-1750s, Kant criticizes arguments for God's existence from the apparent order and design in the universe. This critique has some consistent features across Kant's whole development, and is rooted not in lack of belief, or a confidence in "science versus religion" but in a theological critique of an erroneous doctrine of God, which emphasizes the divine will, and a subsequent misunderstanding of the nature of matter. Kant's argument in 1763 is that the order and harmony that we find in the laws of nature do not depend upon the intervening and designing will of God, but upon the order that is inherent to uncreated essences, structured, as we have seen, by the real possibilities that are grounded in the divine understanding.

The natural theologian looks for evidence of the existence of God on the basis of order in nature. As early as 1755 Kant complains that such natural theology assumes, wrongly, that the "admirable adaptation" we see in the world must be "foreign to nature" left to its own resources, and that nature "abandoned to its own general laws . . . would bring forth nothing but disorder" (*UNH*, 1: 223). Rather, Kant writes, nature is "bound to certain necessary laws":

> Matter, which is the primitive constituent of all things is therefore bound to certain laws, and when it is freely abandoned to these laws it must necessarily bring forth beautiful combinations. It has no freedom to deviate from this perfect plan. (*UNH,* 1: 227-28)

Natural theology, Kant worries, presumes that such order could only arise by virtue of some sort of divine "special government" (*UNH*, 1: 224; see also *OPA,* 2: 123-36). In contrast, Kant insists that the orderliness of nature is sustained not by the intervention of the divine will, but by the "common origin" of the essences that underlie nature in an "Infinite Intelligence, an Understanding" (*UNH*, 1: 225).

It is this common origin that ensures that nature unfolds in an orderly way, according to "its inherent essential striving" (*UNH,* 1: 226). This orderly unfolding is itself "the most splendid evidence of its dependence on that pre-existing Being who contains in Himself not only the source of these beings themselves but their primary laws of action" (*UNH*, 1: 226).

The natural theologian fears that if nature is in itself "orderly," without the need for divine intervention, then there will be no need to invoke God as an explanatory principle. Kant is reassuring on this front. The reason we do not need to invoke the divine will, he explains, is precisely because nature is grounded in the divine understanding. "Reasons which, as used in the hands of opponents, are dreaded as prejudicial," because they seem to remove the need for the divine will, "are rather in themselves powerful weapons by which to combat them," because the redundancy of the divine will arises from the explanatory power of the divine understanding (*UNH*, 1: 225). Kant's critique of natural theology is subtle: nature does not need the divine will, but only because it is grounded in the divine understanding. "There is a God," Kant argues, "just because nature even in chaos cannot proceed otherwise than regularly and according to order" (*UNH*, 1: 228).

This helps to disrupt a standard narrative, which tells that the rise of science pushes out God. The true picture is more like this: the rise of science, in its first dawn-light, makes a particular conception of God all the more urgent. The divine *will* has to do a lot of work intervening in a blandly meaningless and mechanistic universe, in order to create even the level of order and harmony that manifests itself to our senses, and which provides the raw data for our scientific observations. Kant never has this problem, because he understands that order is intrinsic to matter, where this order depends upon the divine understanding, not the divine will. As a result, Kant is able to reject the need for an intervening, designing God. Kant helps us to see that in some respects, the medieval and the contemporary mindset have more in common with each other, than either do with a particular blip of early modern thought.

All that said, there is a difference between Kant in the 1760s and in the 1780s. As we have seen, Kant in his early thought did consider that we could arrive at knowledge about God on the basis of thinking about possibility as such: that there is something (even a possibility) rather than nothing entails that there is a necessary being. We no longer have such knowledge. Nonetheless, by a route other than knowledge, Kant will return to us everything that we might have thought was lost. Kant no longer claims to know about God, but to believe in God without knowledge. He even claims to prefer things this way, and to find it "providential" that

God only permits us to approach him thus. Kant tells us we should "thank heaven" that "our faith is not knowledge":

> For divine wisdom is apparent in the very fact that we do not know but rather ought to believe that a God exists. (*LPR,* 28: 1084)

By now, we have our answer to the question, "what can I know?" We know about the concept of God, what God would be if there were a God, but we do not know whether or not God exists. On then to our second and third questions: "what should I do?" and "what can I hope?" My real interest in this chapter is in the third question, "what can I hope?" I will claim that the God in whom we must hope is the God of theological rationalism. We cannot get to this answer without going through the second question, "what should I do?" Kant's answer to this question will be: I should strive to be good, and to follow the moral law. We need, therefore, to understand the relationship between the answers to the second and third questions ("strive to be good," and "believe in God").

Kant will claim that in some sense it is crucial to believe in God, in order to secure the possibility of morality.[4] Many commentators have found the relationship between these aspects of Kant's thought, goodness and God, to be obscure and insecure, or even disastrous and self-contradictory. I will say more about these rival interpretations a little later, after having set out my interpretation. I want, first of all, to try to show that there is a way of reading Kant whereby his account of what it is to "strive to be good" obviously cries out for, and tips over into, some sort of belief in God. To facilitate this, we need to explore some aspects of what Kant means by "striving to be good" (although a full account is deferred to the final chapter); and to do that, I need to open up some textures in ways in which we come to believe something. Here we come, in my view, to one of the most surprising gifts from Kant to theology. Kant is subtle, filigreed, and textured about the different ways in which we "hold for true" *(Für-wahrhalten)* a range of propositions and commitments, ordered to various aspects of rational human endeavor, not all of which can be reduced to the task of knowing facts.

I might say that "I believe that 2 + 2 = 4," that "murder is wrong," and that "I am now in Oxford." We use the same word, "believe," but quite dif-

4. Some of the material on pp. 34-40 has appeared in my article "Kant on God and the Good: Hoping for Happiness," *Challenging Religious Issues* 8 (2015): 8-12.

ferent routes are taken in each case when assenting to these propositions: mathematical necessity in the first case, a normative moral assertion in the second, and a description in the third. All of these are reasonable beliefs, but my reason is being employed in different ways. Thinking about the different textures of reason will help us to grasp a central feature of Kant's critical philosophy.

Fundamentally, for Kant, human reason is involved in a single and unified encounter with reality. Nonetheless, this single encounter has different aspects, along the lines just explored. In particular, and going back to a central Aristotelian distinction, reason can be involved with knowing, or with making and doing. When reason is concerned with knowing, Kant calls this reason in its theoretical (or speculative) capacity, or more briefly, "theoretical reason." When reason is concerned with what we should do or make, we call this reason in its practical capacity, or more briefly, "practical reason."

I want to unpack here the use of the word "should" in the statement above, that practical reason informs us what we *should* do or make. Practical reason is a large silo of a concept, and includes all thinking toward an end. The structure of practical reasoning is simple: if you want to achieve this end, do this. If you want to make this, make it like so. If you want to be an effective burglar, become good at picking locks. If you want to be an excellent tennis player, practice every day. But now imagine that the end I want to achieve is to be "good," to become what it is that I ought to be. In the terms set out in the last chapter, to approach the "highest good," to flourish in our properly ordered rational human nature, which leads to harmony, community, and happiness. Kant is centrally concerned with the strand of practical reasoning ordered to the achievement of this end. Hence practical reason is oriented to what we ought to do if we want to be good, and to express our fundamental rational nature.

The distinction between practical and theoretical reason responds to a fairly intuitive notion accessible to most of us. I could pile up lists of "facts" in the process of describing a situation according to theoretical reason: from descriptions of brain synapses to accounts of molecular structure, atmospheric conditions, and social and political history. But no matter how high I build the fact mountain, I might not reach a normative conclusion, one that tells me what ought to be done or avoided, for example, that "torture is wrong." For this, I need reason operating according to its practical aspect ("what we should do"); practical reason will attend carefully to what theoretical reason tells it about a situation, but it also has something to tell theoretical reason.

At this point, it is worth reflecting a little on a feature of Kant's philosophical method. He does not ask, as Descartes does, "do I know anything at all?" or "can I believe anything at all?" and then attempt to build up from ground zero. Rather, Kant starts with fairly robust knowledge claims, or beliefs, and asks, "what would need to be in place for this knowledge claim to be possible?" or "what would need to be in place for this presupposition or belief to be possible?" Kant's first *Critique* begins with the question of what would need to be in place for a certain sort of knowledge claim to be possible (for example, judgments about casually related objects in space). His *Groundwork of the Metaphysics of Morals* asks not whether or not we should want to be good, but simply what *is* "good without limitation" (*GW*, 4: 394), that will finally bring about "the satisfaction of reason" (*GW*, 4: 463).

Kant begins with the assumption that we ought to want to be good (whatever that means), and that we do want to be good, and that being good is the true expression of our essential nature, which is to be rational. We should recall how a theological rationalist thinks about essential natures. We saw in the previous chapter that everything stretches out fully to express its nature, and does this in a glorious harmony with other created things, and with the harmonious order in the universe that finds its origin in the divine nature. What would it be like, then, if we were able to express our true rational nature? Because our true nature, Kant thinks, is to be good, our expressing our true rational nature would mean always willing the good, without let or hindrance, and without temptation or contrary impulses.

The theological rationalist, we remember, is deeply concerned with the ordered harmony in the universe. Just so, in a universe where all human beings desire and will the good, there would be a wonderful harmony between all rational beings, all willing and moving toward the same ends. There would be a community of rational beings, everyone willing ends that could be willed by everyone else. In this glorious vision, all rational beings perfectly become what they ought to be, in a harmonious community with other rational beings, and with God: this, for the theological rationalist, is *happiness*. Nothing else counts as proper *happiness*. Is it the case that rational beings, in this picture, are striving toward happiness, in that they *seek* the state of happiness as their goal? Well, no, not directly. They seek to be good, by willing that which can be universally willed by everyone. Happiness, though, is the sure and certain consequence of this harmonious and universal willing.

When Kant talks, as he does, about the "highest good" as the end of morality, he has in mind such a conception: whereby people always and everywhere will to be good, and as a consequence of this, there is properly ordered happiness. *"Happiness,"* Kant tells us, is

> The state of a rational being in the world in the whole of whose existence *everything goes according to his wish and will.* (*CPrR*, 5: 124)

The key qualification here is that happiness is the state where everything goes not according to any old "wish and will," but according to the "wish and will" of a "rational being" in relation to the "whole" of his existence. "He is worthy of happiness," Kant writes, whose "actions are directed to harmony" with those actions which other rational beings would desire. When the whole is functioning properly, with everyone willing what they ought in community with everyone else, then "from the whole," "the happiness of each part" is guaranteed (*R* 7058). Repeatedly Kant talks of the purpose of morality as a harmonious willing of universal happiness:

> Morality consists in the laws of the generation of true happiness from freedom in general. (*R* 7199, 19: 272-73)

> Morality is grounded on the idea of universal happiness from free conduct. (*R* 6958, 19: 213-14; 1776-78)

> Insofar as human beings really judge in accordance with moral principles. (Happiness would be the natural consequence of that.) (*R* 1171, 1772-75; 15: 518)

Kant's conception of the highest good encompasses two components. First of all, there is the demand that we follow the "supreme principle" (*CPrR*, 5: 110), which is the moral law, the "condition which is itself unconditioned" (*CPrR*, 5: 110). Second, *"happiness* is also required" (*CPrR*, 5: 110). This happiness must be more than just a Stoic self-content with being virtuous, merely present in "partial eyes" (*CPrR*, 5: 110). Rather, the happiness that belongs to the "complete good" must be present even "in the judgement of the impartial reason" (*CPrR*, 5: 110). Universal happiness is the true consequence and end of morality, where "happiness" involves everyone always willing the good, in harmony with all other wills.

As things currently stand for us, the highest good is by no means realized. It is not the case that everybody recognizes the "supreme" principle of the moral law, and those who do are by no means rewarded with universal and harmonious happiness. The history of the world, like the history of each institution, country, or individual, is a history of pride, arrogance, cruelty, self-obsession, vanity, suffering, and loss. Things are not as they "ought to be," on the theologically rationalist conception of how things ought to be: with universal patterns of harmony and consequent delight. This tips us over into the third guiding question of the chapter: "what can I hope?" It is important that we be able to understand the natural and inevitable momentum toward this question from Kant's answer to the question "what should I do?" The answer to the second question is: "I should do the good, which means to will that which can be harmoniously and universally willed by all people, such that — were all people to do this — happiness would be the inevitable consequence." A deep need for happiness is built into Kant's answer to the second question. The question "what can I hope?" arises naturally from this answer. Can I hope for the happiness that would be the inevitable consequence of all people willing only that which can be harmoniously and universally willed by all people?

When all is said and done, the sharpest response to this question, and the starkest and strongest rebuff to what Kant will next say is that "in the end truth, perhaps, is sad."[5] That is to say, it would be desirable if things worked out differently, such that happiness ensued from moral action; but it does not, or not always, and certainly not forever, and we have no evidence for supposing that it ever will. Part of our moral struggle, our heroism, consists in being good anyway, in making the best of a bad job. I think we now know enough about a certain sort of theological rationalist, to know that this will hardly occur to Kant as a legitimate or required answer. The instinct of the theological rationalist, in common with the deep strand of Platonism that runs through this tradition (about which, more in chapter five), is always to go from less to more, from the imperfect to the perfect, from the shadow to the reality, from the cave to the sunlit garden. Only in the movement from less to more do we achieve anything that looks rationally stable, for the theological rationalist, and for Kant.

So what the theological rationalist will look for, in such a situation, is an account of how we can hope to move from the imperfect to the perfect.

---

5. Paul Claudel, in a letter to Jacques Rivière, October 24, 1907, quoted in Josef Pieper, *Happiness and Contemplation,* trans. Richard and Clara Winston (South Bend, IN: St. Augustine's Press, 1979), p. 31.

In this case: how could we hope to guarantee a universe in which happiness is really possible? What sort of reality would we need to posit to guarantee this possibility? Kant's answer is that it must be a creative mind that is by its nature good, and by its will, the origin of all that exists and the guarantor of all that will be. God's "final end in creating the world," Kant writes in the second *Critique,* is "the *highest good,*" which includes the "condition of being worthy of happiness," met with a proper "participation" in this happiness (*CPrR,* 5: 130).

In 1786 Kant writes that "reason *needs* to assume . . . a supreme intelligence as the highest *independent* good . . . in order to give objective reality to the concept of the highest good" (*OIT,* 8: 139). Kant claims to *know* with "complete certainty" that the purpose of the moral law can only be achieved if "there be a God and a future world," and that "no one else knows of any other conditions" that can guarantee properly ordered happiness (A 829/B 857). "I will inexorably believe," Kant writes, "in the existence of God and a **future life**, and I am sure that nothing can make these beliefs unstable, since my moral principles themselves, which I cannot renounce without becoming contemptible in my own eyes, would thereby be subverted" (A 829/B 857).

The reference to a "future life" arises through the same movement of thought. Clearly, the fulfillment of our moral destiny and our happiness does not occur in any of our lifetimes: none of us always will the good, and we are always surrounded by disharmony, in that others also fail to will the good. It must be the case, if imperfection is to be resolved into perfection, that death is not the end. Kant captures this thought by speaking of our hope for the "immortality of the soul" or "the future world." It is enough, at this point, to unpack this simply as the claim that "death is not the end." Kant does not straightforwardly believe in an "afterlife," as we will see in later chapters; his view is more that our true life always has been out of time altogether.

In answer to the question "Whence then am I?" Kant finds God through the hope that we are required to have, in order to make possible our striving to be good. Belief in God is a facet of reason in its practical use, reason ordered to the question of what we ought to do. Theoretical reason, recall, was not able to deliver the conclusion that God exists. But also recall, in answer to the first question, "what can I know?," that theoretical reason (for Kant) was able to tell us what God would be, if there were a God. Now we are ready to join the two arcs, one from theoretical reason, the other from practical reason. The God who we are required to believe in on the grounds of practical reason is the God of theological rationalism that theoretical reason is able to form the concept of. "Whence then am I?": I am found at the beginning and end of morality, in practical reason.

Practical reason, by answering the question "what can I hope?," after asking "what should I do?," "inexorably leads to the concept of a **single**, most **perfect**, and **rational** primordial being" (A 814/B 842), a being of the "highest perfection," a "highest and all-sufficient being" (A 640/B 668). This brings back in the traditional properties that attach to the mere concept of God, before we have established grounds for believing in the existence of the reality described by this concept. If we go to lesser-known sources, there are passages from the 1780s and 1790s where Kant explores fairly florid implications of his theological rationalism that would not look at all out of place in his earlier work. For example, in *Lectures on the Philosophical Doctrine of Religion,* Kant sets out a full and positive account of how the divine will is determined to create, and to create the "most perfect world" (*LPR,* 28: 1061-62), not by something external to God, but by virtue of God's cognition of his self-sufficiency. God necessarily cognizes himself, and being necessarily the all-sufficient ground of everything possible, God's cognition of his all-sufficiency determines God to bring the world into existence:

> God cognizes himself by means of his highest understanding as the all-sufficient ground of everything possible. He is most well-pleased with his unlimited faculty as regards all positive things, and it is just this well-pleasedness with himself which causes him to make these possibilities actual. (*LPR,* 28: 1061)

In "cognizing himself," Kant tells us, "he cognizes everything possible which is contained in him as its ground," where this "well-pleasedness of a being with itself as a possible ground for the production of things is what determines its causality" (*LPR,* 28: 1061-62), so that the "product of such a will will be the greatest whole of everything possible . . . the most perfect world" (*LPR,* 28: 1061-62).

Kant endorses a similar viewpoint in writings published in 1793, writing that "the cause of God's will consists in the fact that despite his highest self-contentment, things external to him shall exist insofar as he is conscious of himself as an all-sufficient being":

> [the Deity] although subjectively in need of no external thing, still cannot be thought to shut himself up within himself but rather [must be

thought] to be determined to produce the highest good beyond himself just by his consciousness of his all-sufficiency. (*TP*, 8: 280n)

This is theological rationalism in a strongly Platonic key, and Kant is producing it (in both lectures and published works) in the 1780s and 1790s: God delighting in God's nature brings about a world, which is diffusive of God's own goodness and self-delight. It is because, and only because, the world is brought about as such a diffusion of divine delight that we can hope for the harmony between morality and happiness, which hope is required for our moral striving. Here we see again the truth of something noted at the beginning of the chapter: that Kant's religious perspective is not necessarily or straightforwardly Christian. Many Christian theologians might want to hear more about God's freedom whether or not to create the world *ex nihilo*. Where we find close parallels in the Christian tradition to Kant's position is in thinkers also influenced by Platonism, such as Aquinas, who explains that the creation is God's own self-"communication of being" arising from God's own "goodness." Aquinas writes that

This is evident from the very nature and definition of the good ... the good is diffusive of itself and of being. But this diffusion befits God because ... God is the cause of being for other things.[6]

There are other perspectives on Kant's so-called "moral proof for the existence of God," which is the movement of thought that I have set out in answer to Kant's question "what can I hope?" Both defenders and detractors of this movement of Kant's thought tend to hover around a few shared problems, arising from reflection upon the motivation for morality and the content of the moral law. I will say something, briefly, about each area of concern in turn.

In relation to the motivation for being moral, the anxiety can be that belief in God really ought not to be required by Kant, because Kant also wants it to be the case that we act morally not because of "external incentives," but simply because it is the right thing to do. Kant crystallizes this notion of the "purity" of morality in the mid-1780s. Prior to this time, one can find in Kant suggestions that the hope for happiness does, and even should, provide an incentive for being moral (A 813/B 841; *Coll*, 27: 274,

6. Thomas Aquinas, *Summa Contra Gentiles*, trans. and ed. Vernon J. Bourke (Notre Dame: University of Notre Dame Press, 1975), 1.37.

308). The clarification that this must not be the case, and that morality must be motivating by itself, receives its paradigmatic statement in Kant's *Groundwork of the Metaphysics of Morals* in 1785. The suspicion can be that where God remains in Kant's thought after 1785, as the guarantor of happiness, this is an untidy loose end, which Kant ought to have trimmed. Where Kant failed, we, at least, can finish the job of removing such "impure" incentives from morality.

Such a cleaning up of Kant fails to understand conceptual possibilities from within the tradition out of which he thinks. Within this tradition, there is, in fact, no difficulty in simultaneously clarifying the importance of stripping away inadequate incentives, while finding a proper place for happiness. The state of happiness, in the Platonist/rationalist tradition, is never the incentive or the goal of the harmonious rational agent. The incentive is the striving to know the good, to be good, and to will that which is harmonious and universalizable, and which can therefore be willed in community with all rational beings: happiness is the inevitable consequence of this glorious goal having been achieved. Such a structure is familiar in Christian Platonic patterns of thought: for Aquinas, our end is happiness, but it is not our goal. Our goal is to see God in the beatific vision. A necessary consequence of the beatific vision, just as heat is consequent on fire, is delight and happiness. But the happiness was never our incentive: it was God. For Kant, our incentive, or the "object" of our striving, is morality (about which, more in chapter eight). The consequence, if the morality is perfectly achieved, is happiness. Only belief in God can support the hope that we will all harmoniously and universally orient ourselves, entirely and always, to that which is moral. Only such universal and harmonious willing would lead to happiness. For Kant, at least from the mid-1780s, belief in God does not *generate* our motivation for being good. Our moral motivation is built into reason, and into us, inasmuch as we participate in reason.

Similarly, it is clear that Kant's belief in God does not determine the content of morality ("what is the good?"): the "good" is our willing that which can be universally desired by all rational beings, not an arbitrary dictate from a divine dictator. Although Kant talks at points of God *commanding* the moral law, he is clear that it is not God's command that grounds morality.[7] Rather, God *commands* that which is the moral law, precisely

---

7. Here I disagree with John Hare's account of Kant as a kind of divine command theorist about moral obligation. See Hare, "Kant's Divine Command Theory and Its Reception

because it is the moral law, independently of, and prior to, any action of the divine will:

> An action must be done, not because God wills it, but because it is righteous or good in itself; it is because of this that God wills it and demands it of us. (*Coll,* 27: 262)

Criticizing those who derive "morality from the divine will," Kant tells us that although "any moral law" is also a divine command, the moral law does not "flow from such a command":

> God has commanded it because it is a moral law, and His will coincides with the moral law. (*Coll,* 27: 277; see also *Coll,* 27: 283, 302, 307, 309)

Kant's remaining belief in God can be seen to answer a deeper, older, and distinctively religious hope: not just "why am I motivated to follow the moral law?" or "what is the content of the moral law?," but "what is the shape, purpose, and hope of the whole universe within which I find myself stretched out to follow the *moral law?*"[8] In the previous chapter, I argued that Kant, in his own understated way, would participate in the Platonic and rationalist tendency to discern patterns of desire in the universe, from the less complete to the whole, from the less perfect to the perfect. And so we have found it to be.

Kant is often presented as a stern and duty-obsessed figure, who instructs us that we must do the right thing regardless of the consequences and regardless of whether it makes us or others happy. He is presented in numerous ethics textbooks as starkly opposed to moral perspectives that seek happiness. But it would be wrong to say that Kant has no interest in happiness. He is opposed to our striving for partial, selfish, or incomplete forms of happiness. But Kant approves of happiness, holding out a deep hope for it, when happiness is conceived in sufficiently cosmic and universal terms such that everyone is happy for the right reasons.

---

within Analytical Philosophy," in *Kant and Kierkegaard on Religion,* ed. D. Z. Phillips and Timothy Tessin (New York: Palgrave Macmillan, 2000), pp. 263-77; "Kant on Recognizing our Duties as God's Commands," *Faith and Philosophy* 17 (2000): 459-78; *God's Call: Moral Realism, God's Commands, and Human Autonomy* (Grand Rapids: Eerdmans, 2001), pp. 87-119; *God and Morality: A Philosophical History* (Oxford: Wiley-Blackwell, 2009), pp. 122-75.

8. See my "The Irreducible Importance of Religious Hope in Kant's Conception of the Highest Good," *Philosophy* 83.3 (2008): 333-51.

The interpretation of the concept of the "highest good" that I set out here has the advantage of relating various facets of Kant's moral philosophy in a harmonious way. We have done this by giving a generous space to Kant's own theological pronouncements, and by taking Kant at his word when he talks about the relationship between happiness and God, even to the point of explaining, as he does in the second *Critique,* that "happiness" is "God's final end in creating the world" (*CPrR,* 5: 130). In providing a robustly theological interpretation of the highest good, I am not alone.[9] Nonetheless, there are "secular" interpretations of the "highest good" in the secondary literature, which would not give theology such a generous space. Broadly speaking, these take two forms. First of all, Kant can be simply chastised for failing to understand his own system. That is, Kant ought not to have invoked the concept of the highest good, and even if it was important to Kant, it ought not to be important to us. For example, Lewis White Beck writes that "we must not be deceived, as I believe Kant was, into thinking" that the concept of the highest good is "directly necessary to morality," or indeed that it is at all "important in Kant's philosophy for any practical consequences it might have."[10] This line of thought continues to have followers.[11] A second line of secular interpretation insists that the important function of the concept of the highest good is to add content to the moral law by specifying a particular duty for us, that is, to attempt to maximize happiness in proportion to virtue. Kant seems to invoke this sort of notion of the highest good in 1793, when he writes that we "need to assume, as the final end of all things, a good that is the *highest good* in the world," which is "also possible through our cooperation" (*TP,* 8: 280n). We do not need to believe in God in order to attempt to live by such a principle, although language about God might somehow "regulate" our conduct to this end (about which, more below).[12]

---

9. Although there are differences in nuance, I am broadly in agreement with Frederick Beiser, "Moral Faith and the Highest Good," in *The Cambridge Companion to Kant and Modern Philosophy,* ed. Paul Guyer (Cambridge: Cambridge University Press, 2002), pp. 588-629; and with Lawrence Pasternack, "The Development and Scope of Kantian Belief: The Highest Good, The Practical Postulates and The Fact of Reason," *Kant-Studien* 102.3 (2011): 290-315.

10. Lewis White Beck, *Commentary on the Critique of Practical Reason* (Chicago: University of Chicago Press, 1960), p. 245.

11. See Thomas Auxter, "The Unimportance of the Highest Good," *History of Philosophy Quarterly* 17 (1979): 121-34; Lance Simmons, "Kant's Highest Good: Albatross, Keystone, Achilles' Heel," *History of Philosophy Quarterly* 10.4 (1993): 355-68.

12. See John Silber, "Kant's Conception of the Highest Good as Immanent and Tran-

I would say three things in relation to these "secular" approaches to the concept of the highest good. First of all, they are only persuasive if we are prepared to ignore passages from Kant's works that clearly do insist that the highest good is important to his moral philosophy, and that belief in God (and immortality) are essential consequences of hoping for the highest good. We have given clear examples of such passages in the discussion above with evidence from the first two *Critiques,* to which we can add a passage from the third *Critique* (1790), where Kant writes that the "highest good" is "possible" only "under the rule" of a "legislative sovereign in a moral realm of ends" (*CJ,* 5: 444).

Second, theological interpretations of the "highest good" have no difficulty coping with passages, such as that quoted above, where Kant talks of our duty to attempt to bring about happiness proportionate to virtue. If the ultimate end of creation is happiness in proportion to virtue, then *of course* we should do what we can to further this, consonant with our abilities and other duties. This is what we would expect. If bringing about happiness in proportion to virtue were not in some sense, and to some degree, a duty, it would be hard to square with the claim that happiness in proportion to virtue is the final end of creation. This simply reflects the standard and perennial way in which eschatological hope always faces two ways: "thy kingdom come" is a call to action, even though it is an action that we can only participate in, relying and waiting upon the fullness of divine action. The interpretative situation in relation to secular and theological interpretations of the highest good is not a case of having two sorts of irreconcilable texts, where we must make a difficult choice between them: on the one hand, clearly "secular" passages, and, on the other hand, suggestively "theological" passages. The choice is rather between being able to give a good account of *all* the passages, or only a *minority* of passages, notably excluding passages from all three *Critiques.* In this book, and throughout my scholarship, I assume that it is always preferable to seek an interpretation that can incorporate as many passages as possible from texts intended by the author as a unity. On this principle, the theological interpretation of the highest good carries the day.

Although I consider secular interpretations of the "highest good" to be poor at tracking Kant's own intentions, my third comment is more irenic. When all is said and done, secular interpretations of the "highest good" are

---

scendent," *Philosophical Review* 68 (1959): 460-92; Andrews Reath, "Two Conceptions of the Highest Good in Kant," *Journal of the History of Philosophy* 26.4 (1988): 593-619.

onto something. They are at least in the neighborhood of a deep problem in Kant's philosophy, which can in fact become more visible and intense precisely by taking the theology seriously, as I believe Kant did. The problem is how to relate Kant's demands on freedom, with his (genuine) theological hope for the highest good. Kant becomes more aware of this deep tension, certainly in the final years of his life (as I argue in chapter eight), and possibly as early as the 1790s. In this regard, it might indeed be significant that Kant gives the concept of the "highest good" a more immanent and historical spin in 1793, when he talks about it as "possible through our cooperation" (*TP*, 8: 280n). This might reflect a growing awareness on Kant's part that God cannot do the work he was hoping, given his conception of the relationship between divine action and human freedom. Secular interpretations have hit upon something, but for the wrong reasons. The awkwardness of the highest good in Kant's system does not arise because of a lack of commitment to belief in God, but rather because of the precise intra-theological content of what this belief entails for human freedom. Furthermore, Kant's eventual dissolution of the hope for the highest good (tracked in chapter eight) is perhaps post-Christian, harkening back to pre-Christian Platonism, but it is hardly "secular."

Believing "As If" There Is a God

The question of how to interpret Kant's concept of the "highest good" is one flashpoint between theological and secular readings of Kant. There is another related area of controversy, which also needs to be engaged with here. We can grant that Kant refers to "God," and that such passages need to be incorporated into our interpretation. Nonetheless, we can still question the precise status and significance of such references. Many commentators offer a different explanation of the role of God language in Kant's mature philosophy to the one I have offered here.[13] Putting it briskly, the alternative explanation offered is this: in his mature thought, Kant retains the concept of God merely as an "*as if*" belief, inasmuch as this is useful, to either theoretical or practical projects. That is to say, Kant does not really believe in God, but considers that human practices can

---

13. See, for example, James DiCenso, *Kant's Religion within the Boundaries of Mere Reason* (Cambridge: Cambridge University Press, 2012); Peter Byrne, *Kant on God* (Aldershot: Ashgate, 2007); Paul Guyer, *Kant* (London: Routledge, 2006), chaps. 3 and 6.

reap some rewards by retaining the concept, used as a heuristic category, either to motivate us to look for greater degrees of order and systematicity when studying the natural world ("*as if*" there is an intelligent designer), or when understanding the gravity and bindingness of the moral law ("*as if*" it were commanded by a divine legislator), or (in relation to the debate around the highest good) when attempting to bring about happiness in proportion to virtue.

In a sense, this account is not entirely wrong about Kant. But it is also not the whole truth. It is not entirely wrong, in that Kant does indeed have a notion of belief in God that can help to "regulate" our various projects. Such "regulative" belief in God, I agree, does not commit us really to believing in God. An example of a regulative belief might be "the customer is always right." If I am a shop assistant I might accept this statement as regulating my behavior in relation to customers. But I will not, if I am rational, believe it. Customers are often wrong: they tell lies, they have not properly looked after the product they are returning, or they have unreasonable expectations. Kant has such a regulative concept of God up and running in his thought; but it is not all he has, and he is very clear about this. It is worth dedicating some time to this, for two reasons. First of all, the question of whether or not the mature Kant really believes in God is central to this book. Second, the discussion will give further evidence for a key claim of the book: that one of Kant's surprising gifts to theology is his nuance and subtlety in describing different textures of our assent to propositions. Not all rational assent is knowledge, and it is good that it is not.

Toward the end of the first *Critique* Kant differentiates three different types of *Glaube,* or "belief," which can also be translated as "faith." He calls these different types of *Glaube* pragmatic, doctrinal, and moral. Our acceptance that "the customer is always right" is a type of pragmatic *Glaube,* as it helps to regulate our conduct toward a worthy end. Kant gives two examples of his own. First of all, a doctor who needs to make a diagnosis in order to treat an illness (A 824/B 852). The doctor is equally divided between a number of diagnoses, each of which require a different treatment. If the doctor makes no decision, and offers no diagnosis, the patient will certainly die. So the doctor forms a pragmatic belief around a particular diagnosis, and treats accordingly. The doctor accepts a particular diagnosis, and uses this to regulate her actions, although in fact the doctor is no more theoretically committed to the truth of this diagnosis than to any other. In some lectures on logic, Kant gives another example, of a businessman who "in order to strike a deal," needs "not just to opine that there will be something to be gained thereby, but to believe it, i.e., to have his opinion be sufficient for an undertaking into the uncertain" (*JL*, 9: 67-68n).

The second type of *Glaube* that Kant treats he calls "doctrinal belief." This texture of belief is particularly relevant for us, as "the thesis of the existence of God belongs to doctrinal belief" (A 826/B 854). Such a doctrinal belief in God is not committed to the truth of the claim that there is a God, but uses the presupposition in order to support the assumption that there is a "purposive unity" in the universe. This assumption of "purposive unity," Kant considers, is a "condition of the application of reason to nature," where there is no "other condition for this unity" than the presupposition of "a highest intelligence" (A 826/B 854). By embracing an "*as if*" belief in God, my rational project of finding order and harmony in the universe is regulated and nurtured. Kant is clear though that such a belief "concerns only the direction that an idea gives me" (A 827/B 855). It is "contingent" upon my need to have a "guide for the investigation of nature," where the "outcome of my experiments" confirms the "usefulness of this presupposition" (A 826/B 854). Kant calls both pragmatic and doctrinal beliefs "regulative ideas" or "concepts of reason," where we need make no commitment to there being any sort of "object" corresponding to our beliefs, but where we employ such beliefs as "heuristic fictions" (A 771/B 799).

If pragmatic and doctrinal beliefs were the whole story, and belief in God no more than a type of doctrinal belief, then the (once) standard account of Kant would be correct: that he does not really believe in God, but uses the concept in an "*as if*" sense, simply to regulate some of our rational projects. This impression would seem to gain further confirmation from Kant's treatment of historically "revealed" doctrines in *Religion within the Boundaries of Mere Reason,* where doctrines such as atonement and grace (*Rel,* 6: 57-89), incarnation (*Rel,* 6: 60-66), and bodily resurrection (*Rel,* 6: 129) are given rather bracing translations into terms that are useful to practical reason, with any reference to supernatural or divine agency heavily circumscribed, even to the point of being mistrusted.

This is not, though, the whole story. Kant is explicit that there is another texture of *Glaube,* of belief in God, which is of a different order to the pragmatic or the doctrinal. This texture is moral belief in God, that arises from our attempts to be moral, and through morality to achieve the highest good, of which happiness is the consequence. Belief in God that arises from moral considerations, from practical reason with respect to morality and the highest good, is not a type of merely regulative belief.

Kant marks this out by giving it the distinctive status of a "postulate of practical reason" in the second *Critique.* In the first *Critique* Kant insists that doctrinal/regulative belief in God must "not be called practical" (A 827/B 855). The point here is that doctrinal belief in God does not reach the status or stability of practical/moral belief, because "there is something unstable about merely doctrinal beliefs" resulting from "difficulties that come up in speculation" (A 829/B 857). "It is entirely otherwise," Kant insists, "in the case of moral belief":

> For there it is absolutely necessary that something must happen, namely, that I fulfill the moral law in all points. The end here is inescapably fixed, and according to all my insight there is possible only a single condition under which this end is consistent with all ends together and thereby has practical validity, namely, that there be a God and a future world; I also know with complete certainty that no one else knows of any other conditions that lead to this same unity of ends under the moral law. But since the moral precept is thus at the same time my maxim (as reason commands that it ought to be), I will inexorably believe in the existence of God and a future life, and I am sure that nothing can make these beliefs unstable, since my moral principles themselves, which I cannot renounce without becoming contemptible in my own eyes, would thereby be subverted. (A 829/B 857)

Kant makes a similar distinction, between regulative-doctrinal belief in God and practical-moral belief, in his 1786 essay *What Does It Mean to Orient Oneself in Thinking?* (1786). The theoretical and doctrinal need of reason is "only conditioned," which is to say that it is only useful to a particular purpose:

> We must assume the existence of God *if we want to judge* about the first causes of everything contingent, chiefly in the order of ends which is actually present in the world. (*OIT,* 8: 139)

"Far more important," Kant explains, "is the need of reason in its practical use":

> Because it is unconditioned, and we are necessitated to presuppose the existence of God not only if we *want* to judge, but because we *have to judge* . . . reason *needs* to assume . . . a supreme intelligence as the highest

independent good . . . in order to give objective reality to the concept of the highest good, i.e., to prevent it, along with morality, from being taken merely as a mere ideal, as it would be if that whose idea inseparably accompanies morality should not exist anywhere. (*OIT*, 8: 139)

In the second *Critique* Kant explains that practical reason grounds the "objective reality" of God and immortality, as well as freedom. He even goes so far as to explain that through practical reason, theoretical cognition is extended:

Thus by the practical law that commands the existence of the highest good possible in the world, the possibility of those objects of pure speculative reason, the objective reality which the latter could not assure them, is postulated; by this the theoretical cognition of pure reason certainly receives an increment, but it consists only in this: that those concepts, otherwise problematic (merely thinkable) for it, are now declared assertorically to be concepts to which real objects belong, because practical reason is thereby justified in assuming them. (*CPrR*, 5: 134)

Theoretical reason is "forced to grant *that there are such objects*" as God and immortality, "though it cannot determine them more closely and so cannot itself extend this cognition of the objects" (*CPrR*, 5: 135).

Kant returns to the distinction between merely regulative beliefs, and belief based on morality, in his 1793 essay *What Real Progress Has Metaphysics Made in Germany?* Kant denies, as we would expect, that we can have "theoretical knowledge" beyond "objects of the senses" (*WRP*, 20: 296). But he goes on to insist that the "modality of our assent" to the proposition that there is a God is neither a case of opinion nor probability (*WRP*, 20: 297). The "super-sensible differs in its very species from the sensuously knowable," so that there is "no way at all of reaching it by those very same steps whereby we may hope to arrive at certainty in the field of the sensible":

Thus there is no approximation to it either, and therefore no assent whose logical value could be called probability. (*WRP*, 20: 299)

When it comes to God, Kant explains, we must have "*belief*" (*WRP*, 20: 297), which is "not a prudential doctrine" along the lines that it is "better to believe to profess too much than too little" (*WRP*, 20: 298). In such a case Kant complains, "the belief would not be sincere" (*WRP*, 20: 298). Rather, belief in God, freedom, and immortality is "necessary" in "a moral sense," whereby we "grant them objective reality" (*WRP*, 20: 299).

Practical reason leads us to robust belief in the God of theological rationalism. It is against this context that we should understand Kant's project in *Religion within the Boundaries of Mere Reason*. Kant explains that the aim of the work is to translate from the "outer circle" of historically revealed doctrine, into the "inner circle" of practical reason (*Rel*, 6: 12). This "inner circle" can be too quickly read as a secular form of practical reason, with no genuine belief in God. But this is not what Kant says. He calls the "inner circle" the sphere of the "pure *religion of reason*" (*Rel*, 6: 12). The "historically revealed doctrine" found in the outer sphere is largely framed in a Lutheran vocabulary, with an emphasis upon Christ's vicarious atonement for our sins, which leads to our being reckoned as righteous. Kant does not translate this into secular terms, but, as he himself says, into the "pure *religion of reason*" (*Rel*, 6: 12), which, I have suggested, is a variant of theological rationalism, warranted on the basis of our orientation toward the good, as expressed in practical reason. It is a translation from one theological discourse (historical Lutheranism) into another, for Kant, more fundamental theological discourse (rationalism with strong Platonic strands). So, for example, the Lutheran notion of Christ dying for our sins is taken to symbolize our own self-transcendence, as we go beyond our selfish self-assertion and orient ourselves instead to that which can be universally and harmoniously willed by all. The "sacrifice," the "crucifying of the flesh," stands for our 'emergence from the corrupted disposition into the good," where the "new human being" shares the "disposition of the Son of God" by acting "simply for the sake of the good" (*Rel*, 6: 74).

The incarnation, whereby God sends his son to redeem us from our sins, is given a remarkably and frankly Platonic explanation. The incarnation points to "*humanity* (rational being in general as pertaining to the world) *in its full moral perfection,* from which happiness follows in the will of the Highest Being directly as from its supreme condition" (*Rel*, 6: 60). This "ideal of moral perfection" is "the prototype of moral disposition in its entire purity" (*Rel*, 6: 61):

> This human being, alone pleasing to God, "is in him from all eternity"; the idea of him proceeds from God's being; he is not, therefore, a created thing but God's only-begotten Son, "the *Word*" (the *Fiat!*) through

which all other things are, and without whom nothing that is made would exist (since for him, that is, for a rational being in the world, as can be thought according to its moral determination, everything was made). — "He is the reflection of his glory." — "In him God loved the world," and only in him and through the adoption of his dispositions can we hope "to become children of God." (*Rel*, 6: 60-61)

We need to be clear here precisely what is the subject of the translation, and what the product. That which is being translated is the biblical (especially Johannine) and traditional language of a divine "union with us" affected by the "*abasement* of the Son of God," who has been sent down "to us from heaven" and "taken up humanity" in the historical figure of Jesus (*Rel*, 6: 61). What such historical doctrine points to, for Kant, is the idea of the "human being conforming to [the] prototype" of "moral perfection." Such a "prototype" has, from a practical point of view, "complete reality within itself," as it "resides in our morally-legislative reason" (*Rel*, 6: 62). The significance of saying that the "prototype" comes "down from heaven" and takes on humanity is that "we are not [the] authors" of the idea of moral perfection, but rather that this idea has "established itself in the human being without our comprehending how human nature could have ever been receptive of it" (*Rel*, 6: 61). This category of moral perfection belongs within the sphere of the "pure *religion of reason*" (*Rel*, 6: 12), and is not itself a mere heuristic fiction. Such a concept of moral perfection, as we have seen, makes further demands on our thought, requiring belief in God and in immortality. The serviceable "fiction" which Kant translates is not the reality of the prototype, but rather the notion that an historical individual called Jesus is in fact to be identified with this ideal prototype.[14]

All can agree that in *Religion within the Boundaries of Mere Reason*, Kant translates historical doctrine into the terms of practical reason. This in itself is not yet to say very much. Everything turns on what we think the "terms of practical reason" are. If I am correct that practical reason leads Kant to substantive theological commitments, the translation into practical reason will be a translation from one theological discourse into another, and not from the religious into the secular. The translation certainly puts

---

14. For a discussion of the notion of the prototype, to which I am indebted here, see Nathan Jacobs, "Kant's Prototypical Theology: Transcendental Incarnation as a Rational Foundation for God-Talk," in *Kant and the New Philosophy of Religion*, ed. Chris L. Firestone and Stephen R. Palmquist (Bloomington: University of Indiana Press, 2006), pp. 124-40.

Kant in a strained relationship with traditional Christianity, but it is still a type of theology, in that it makes claims about God and our relation to God.

As explained above, theoretical and practical reason are not two distinct "faculties," but are facets of a single reason engaged with the questions: "(1.) What can I know? (2.) What should I do? (3.) What can I hope?" (A 805/B 833). When discussing the primacy of practical reason in moral contexts, Kant writes about "the union of pure speculative with pure practical reason in one cognition," where theoretical reason "must accept" propositions that "*belong inseparably to the practical interest* or pure reason" (*CPrR,* 5: 121). Theoretical reason must recognize its shared nature with practical reason:

> It is still only one and the same reason which, whether from a theoretical or a practical perspective, judges according to a priori principles. (*CPrR,* 5: 121)

This theme of the unity of reason is also picked up in the *Groundwork,* where Kant writes that "there can, in the end, be only one and the same reason, which must be distinguished merely in its application" (*GW,* 4: 391). This brings us to another of the promised gifts from Kant to theology: his appreciation of the patterned dynamism and unity of reason. Reason undertakes different tasks, using a range of incommensurate criteria. Nonetheless, reason aspires to a fundamental unity. One facet of reason can offer gifts to another, where each expression of reason must study its limitations, and its need and ability to receive. We have seen something of this reciprocal dance of needs in this chapter: theoretical reason can deliver us the concept of God, but cannot know that God exists. Practical reason informs reason in its theoretical use of the existence of God. The pattern goes through another cycle in the third *Critique,* as theoretical reason receives support in its understanding of nature, through its assumption, given resonance by assurances from morality, that there are teleological patterns of order in nature. Swirling back again, this theoretical interest (falling short of knowledge) in teleology ("physical ends") in nature provides further support for our moral interest in God:

> Now the objective reality of the idea of God as the moral author of the world cannot of course be established by means of physical ends **alone**; nevertheless, if the cognition of those ends is connected with that of the moral end, then the former, because of the maxim of pure reason to seek

unity of principles as far as possible, is of great significance for assisting the practical reality of that idea by means of the reality that it already has for the power of judgment from a theoretical point of view. (*CJ,* 5:456)

The next four chapters will, explicitly and implicitly, offer further support for the claim developed in this chapter, that Kant continues to believe in God throughout the 1780s and (most of) the 1790s. In these chapters, we will see that Kant worries about fairly technical and traditional issues in relating God to the creation. Kant will claim that God is not the creator of things within space and time (*CPrR,* 5: 102), that space is "not a thing as a divine work" (*R* 6057, 18: 439), that God does not concur with free human action (I will explain "concur"). All of these claims arise in the context of Kant's struggle with our opening questions: how to relate our freedom, our ability to do other than the good, with our calling to perfection (to the highest good), and how to believe in a God who can guarantee our achievement of perfection, and the happiness consequent upon this, without thereby believing in a God who makes freedom impossible for us.

Kant deals extensively and continuously with the question of the precise causal joint between God and the creation. This is a significant and important problem, if Kant really does believe in God. It is less easy to see why such technical issues matter, to Kant, if he simply employs the concept of God on an "as if" basis, where he works on the heuristic assumption that there is a God, but without really believing in God. Put simply: for Kant, belief in God can be a nuisance. If we were going to make up beliefs simply because they were useful, we might not start here.

Conclusion

Drawing together the two chapters given so far, my key claim has been that Kant believed in God throughout his whole development, excepting perhaps the final few years (to be discussed in the final chapter). Kant's concept of God is saturated in the categories of theological rationalism. Such a God is the ground of all real possibilities, or essences. These essences constitute the divine understanding. God delights in his own nature, in his self-sufficiency, harmony, goodness, and perfection. This delight is diffusive of itself, bringing about the creation, as God wills to express the goodness of the divine nature. In Kant's early thought, he considered that he could prove the existence of such a God to the satisfaction of reason in its theoretical capacity. In his later thought, he becomes convinced that he cannot prove the existence of God by theoretical reason, but that we are warranted and required to believe in God on moral and practical grounds. What Kant believes in remains remarkably stable; how he comes to this belief shifts significantly.

The problem to be explored in the next two chapters is that although keeping God in the picture provides a way to guarantee the goods of moral perfection and the consequent happiness, the same God threatens our capacity to be free, which Kant comes to regard as regrettably essential to moral perfection. Chapter four will show how the crisis of relating human freedom to God unfolds for Kant in the 1760s and 1770s. Chapter five will set out how Kant solves this problem, almost (but not quite) to his own satisfaction, at least for a time.

CHAPTER FOUR

Kant's "Only Unsolvable Metaphysical Difficulty": Created Freedom

Imagine yourself newly married, and a citizen of present-day Kaliningrad, a seaport city on the Russian Baltic coast. One morning, soon after your wedding, you and your partner might, by force of local custom and expectation, find yourselves making your way to a revered tomb in the precincts of the cathedral. You are carrying a wreath of flowers. The tomb is easily identifiable, already strewn with floral offerings, and bearing the engraved words, in both German and Russian:

> Two things fill the mind with ever new and increasing admiration and reverence, the more often and more steadily one reflects on them: *the starry heavens above me and the moral law within me.*

This is Immanuel Kant's tomb. The once Prussian city of Königsberg is renamed Kaliningrad in 1946, when it is incorporated in the Soviet empire. Upon the site of the Castle under which Kant's house used to stand we now find the brutally modernist House of Soviets. Kant's tomb has become a sort of shrine for newlyweds, rather in the style of a local orthodox saint. Commentators typically note a certain irony here: Kant had a very low threshold for what he regarded as "superstition" (with church services as such being suspect).[1]

At the same time, though, I want to say that there is something apropos about the scene just imagined. The unfolding drama of Kant's thought is the struggle between our freedom to do what we want, and so to do

---

1. See Allen W. Wood, "Kant's Life and Works," in *A Companion to Kant* (Oxford: Wiley-Blackwell, 2010), pp. 10-29 (p. 10).

other than the good, and our constantly renewed and frustrated efforts to be what we ought to be (expressed by Kant's notion of the highest good), and so to reach a properly ordered happiness. Arguably, marriage is one theater of human life where we bind ourselves to a good that is higher than our fleeting desires and impulses, and from deeper freedom bind ourselves to a law that we give ourselves. The "moral law within me," whereby I attach myself to what it is I ought to be, can be frustrated both by my own acts and omissions, but also by external events, tragedies, and loss. Our freedom, efforts, and hopes can be erased by my own failures, but also by the fates embodied in "the starry heavens."

This takes us back to the words on Kant's tomb, which are from his second *Critique,* published in 1788. The epitaph is an extract from a longer thought, where Kant comments that when reflecting on the heavens and the moral law

> I do not need to search for them and merely conjecture them as though they were veiled in obscurity or in the transcendent region beyond my horizon; I see them before me and connect them immediately with the consciousness of my existence. (*CPrR,* 5: 161-62)

What does it mean to say that both the "moral law" *and* "the starry heavens" are not in a "transcendent region beyond my horizon," but are connected "immediately with the consciousness of my existence"? Contained here is a deep Kantian drama. Kant comes to the point, with increasing urgency through the 1760s and 1770s, where he has to sort out the problem of the starry heavens, in order to secure what he comes to think that freedom requires. What then is the problem presented by the starry heavens? Going back to the passage from the second *Critique,* the source of the epitaph, Kant goes on to tell us that the starry heavens constitute "an unbounded magnitude with worlds upon worlds and systems of systems," such that

> The view of a countless multitude of worlds annihilates, as it were, my importance as an *animal creature,* which after it has been for a short time provided with vital force (one knows not how) must give back to the planet (a mere speck in the universe) the matter from which it came. (*CPrR,* 5: 162)

The starry heavens are like a great machine, teeming with forces, moving with iron patterns of causal determinism. In his mature critical thought (in the 1780s and beyond), Kant comes to the view that freedom requires independence from any external and determining causes. This chapter sets out this gathering crisis in Kant's thought, which is part of what tips him into his so-called "critical philosophy." The next chapter lays out Kant's own solution to this crisis.

The solution that I will set out in the next chapter is this: at a fundamental level of our existence, so fundamental that we can never directly experience it, we are each of us non-spatial and non-temporal. This is where our freedom and our moral struggle *really* happens: in a non-spatial and non-temporal realm, of which our temporal biographies are in some sense derivative appearances. Now, most people do not find this an attractive and gripping account of our attempts to be moral, all of which unfold for us in time and space: I make a promise, and then I keep it; I repent of my dissipated existence, and then I attempt to do better; I grow in virtue by forming my character through good acts. Space and time are for human beings home. We are so bound up with space and time that beings outside of space and time could have no relevant resemblance to us. By the end of the next chapter, I hope that Kant's "solution" to the problem of how to relate our freedom and the moral law within to the starry heavens without will fall off the page as an elegant and satisfying solution, or, at least, as an obvious and luminous solution for Kant, given his wider assumptions.

It is not possible to effect such a transformation of our attitudes without some pain. If Kant is to be our Virgil, the way to paradise will be through purgatory. We need to climb the same slopes that Kant treads, really to understand his solution to the problem of freedom under the starry heavens. Across this chapter and the next we will climb four ledges: two in this chapter, two in the next. On the first ledge, we will come to understand why Kant in his earliest thought has no problem in relating our freedom with the vastness of the created starry heavens. This is because, in the 1750s, Kant is convinced that our actions can be entirely determined, and yet still count as "free," because freedom does not require our ability to do other than we do, and does not require us to be ultimately responsible for our actions. On the second ledge, we find Kant stumbling, anxious and confused, as he begins to raise his eyes toward a more ambitious conception of freedom, which he is entirely unable to comprehend or explain. The problem of how a created soul can be free, Kant reports in the 1770s, is the "only unsolvable metaphysical difficulty."

The characters and concepts we meet on the first ledge present quite a challenge. We will come across Leibniz and Newton in a strange double act, spinning out a universe made up of Leibnizian non-temporal and non-spatial substances, along with Newtonian physical forces of attraction and repulsion. Kant's ascent up the mountain is more like a curved path around a spiral than a linear climb. Kant manages to find his way through the difficulties that beset him on the second ledge, but he does so by digging deep into Platonic strands in his rationalist intellectual heritage, and by recalling, while reconfiguring, what he had learned from Newton and Leibniz (among others) on the first ledge. We need to learn all we can from the first ledge, both to understand the nature of Kant's emerging crisis, *and* to understand how Kant overcomes the same crisis. This is, as set out earlier in the introduction, a characteristic and moving feature of Kant's way of thinking, which is to arrive at solutions by digging deeper, and deeper still, and then a bit more, into the source of the problem, and then the problem with the problem.

Dante and Virgil begin their climb up the mountain of purgatory by "glimpsing four stars/unseen by mortals since the first mankind" (*Purgatorio*, Canto I, lines 23-24). We begin our journey with an imagined glimpse of the first conceptual moments of creation. This will represent Kant's account of the creation as he sets it out in the 1750s. From this, we will be able to understand where Kant thinks our, at this stage determined, freedom fits in. We will see that even in Kant's early thought, freedom and something related to Kant's later conception of the "highest good" are not synonymous. In his early thought, freedom is ordered toward the good that rational human beings ought to will. Some human beings achieve this, and others do not, although all are in a sense "free."

Kant's Account of the Creation in the 1750s

In chapters two and three, we looked at Kant's conception of God, which I argued was saturated in the categories of theological rationalism. In the divine understanding we find the real possibilities of all things, the possible essences of everything that ever could be, existing in a beautiful harmony in the divine mind. From this depository of essences, God chooses that some of these harmonious and ordered essences will be instantiated in the created universe. I want us now to conceive of ourselves as standing before this God and under the nothingness that pre-exists the creation. Imagine a sort of vast conceptual planetarium, upon which we will watch a simulation of the creation of the universe unfold.

In the first conceptual moment of creation, discrete and isolated substances flash onto the screen of our planetarium. What are these "substances"? First and foremost, they are instantiations of the "essences" that I talked about in the first two chapters. An "essence," we recall, is the ordering principle of a reality, that which makes it what it is, and governs how it relates to other things. Essences, therefore, are highly structured with potential patterns of order and lawfulness. Imagine then Leibniz on the first ledge, moving around what appear to be beautiful shining spheres. These spheres represent what Leibniz, and those who follow him, consider to be the fundamental furniture of the universe — unchanging, indivisible, incorruptible substances, each of which instantiates and exemplifies an essence, which is itself an eternal truth held in the divine understanding.

Leibniz and his followers (including Kant) are convinced that space and time, whatever they are, are bound up with that which changes, with that which can be divided, and with that which is corruptible, in the sense that "all flesh is grass," and all things pass away. The fundamental substances of the universe, Leibniz tells the group, cannot therefore be ultimately spatial or temporal, not if they are to be unchanging, indivisible, and incorruptible. Leibniz goes on to insist that these fundamental substances, if they are incorruptible and unchangeable, cannot be impacted by other substances; because, if they were impacted, they would be changed. In the inner circle of Leibniz's followers, nodding at almost everything, are figures such as Baumgarten and Wolff; Kant sits on the outer edges of the group. Sitting next to Kant is his former teacher, Martin Knutzen. Kant nods in agreement that substances cannot fundamentally be spatial and temporal, but, as we will see, both Kant and Knutzen shake their heads in disagreement when Leibniz insists that fundamental substances are therefore unchangeable and not impacted by other substances.

The conclusion that Kant and the Leibnizians all agree on, that the fundamental furniture of the universe consists of non-spatial and non-temporal substances, might seem peculiar and extravagant to those saturated in the observational method of modern science: how do such non-spatial and non-temporal substances enter into the picture if we can never (by definition) observe them, and if we can make reliable empirical predictions without recourse to such entities? To the theological rationalist, though, there is nothing peculiar or extravagant at all in recourse to non-spatial and non-temporal substances. It is *obvious* to the rationalist, as obvious as the observational method to a modern scientist, that to explain that which is changeable, we must make recourse to the unchanging; and that patterns of explanation go from that which is imperfect to that which is perfect, from that which is transient to that which is eternal.

At the same time, theological rationalists, such as Leibniz and Kant, are not crazy. They see the same world that the empiricist sees, and understand that this world appears to be thoroughly spatial and temporal, with the patterns of corruption, generation, and degeneration that come with this. They are not in constant denial about this, or repeatedly scratching their heads, "well blow me, that cheese has gone off, and there was I, thinking that substances were fundamentally non-spatial and non-temporal." So what does the rationalist say about the world in its spatial and temporal appearance? There is simply no problem here for the rationalist. Deep in the bones of any worldview that has a family resemblance to Platonism is the insight, going back to Plato himself, that the ways in which things appear to be, the shadows on the cave wall, are quite different from the way things fundamentally are, the eternal forms. Also, the way that things appear to be, although a flickering and illusory shadow, depends entirely upon the way things really are, albeit that we see the shapes of things through the flames of our cavernous jail. The rationalist, then, is hardly surprised that things appear quite different from the way they really are: "of course they do, that is the whole point," we might say.

Now we can understand how Newton has been invited around our purgatory campfire, with Leibniz and Kant. The way things appear is quite different from the way things fundamentally are. But the way things appear is important: it is the only direct access we have to the way things are. It is vital to understand the nature and structure of these appearances, the way in which the world presents itself. The way in which the world presents itself, the rationalists on our ledge are convinced, is thoroughly Newtonian. By their own lights, they have no difficulty reconciling a fundamental rationalist reality with a thoroughly Newtonian description of what appears to us, or to use the technical term employed by Leibniz, "phenomena," which means, simply, "that which appears."

Up to this point, all the rationalists around our campfire would nod in broad agreement. But if we go on to ask them just *how* the Newtonian phenomena arise from the fundamental reality, and what exactly the status of these Newtonian "appearances" is, then we will soon have a dust-up. Each of the thinkers, Leibniz, Baumgarten, Wolff, and others, have their own particular version of how the Newtonian phenomena arise, and what precisely they are. That in itself tells you quite a lot about the difficulty of knowing what the relationship between the underlying rationalist furniture and Newtonian appearances might be. And this lack of agreement, and the lack of clear means of arriving at agreement, begins really to bother Kant once he is higher up the mountain. All we need to learn from the first ledge, after noting the lack of consensus, is how Kant himself construes the relationship between rationalist substances and Newtonian forces. Kant's version will be just one variation on a theme, and part of a (squabbling) family of related theories, which are hard to adjudicate between.

At some point in the evening then, Kant has had enough, and takes it upon himself to explain to the other Newtonian rationalists just how things work. Stepping up, Kant seizes the beautiful shining spheres from Leibniz. Explaining that the spheres represent created (non-spatial and non-temporal) substances, Kant tells us that in the first conceptual moment of creation, God simply creates the substances, isolated from one another, with no relations between the substances. As the fire flickers on the silver spheres, Kant takes one in each hand, and begins to move them in relation to one another. In the second moment of creation, Kant explains, God freely decides to place these substances in relation with one another. The relations that God sets up between the created substances are in fact, Kant explains, the forces of attraction and repulsion that are described accurately in Newtonian physics. Here there would be a near universal groan of dissent from the group, except for the quietly nodding Knutzen. Substances, Kant insists, against a wave of disapproval, really do impact one another. Kant continues: Newtonian physics describes the relations between created substances. Space and time, Kant explains, are "constituted by the interconnected actions of substances" (*NE*, 1: 415). What is time? It is a product of the relationship that arises, for example, from the forces that run between substances being impacted. What is space? It is the product of the relations between created substances.

From our evening around the campfire with the "rationalists for Newton" support group, I want us to note, and put in the memory bank, three things at this stage. First of all, in the bones of eighteenth-century rationalism, and common to all variants and derivations of Platonism, we have a distinction between that which appears, in the sense of presenting itself both to our senses and to our scientific observations, and that which underlies appearances, fundamentally grounding them, without "resembling" them in any way at all. I will argue that Kant's eventual critical distinction between "phenomena," or "that which appears," and "noumena," or "that which underlies the appearance," is one variation on this deep Platonic theme.

The second thing to note is this. Kant postulates that space and time are not absolute features of the created universe, empty receptacles into which created things pop into being. Rather, space and time are products of the relationship between substances. This will remain a continuous feature of Kant's philosophy right into his critical thought, but the sort of relationship that space and time are a product of will shift: from being a product of their relationship with each other as created by God, to being a product of their relationship with us, as created by God.

The final thing to note is this: one of the questions that propels Kant into his "critical philosophy" is "how do I know about the relationship between the Newtonian appearances and the underlying (rationalist) reality?" This is an especially sharp question given the disagreement around our philosophical campfire, which seems to be in principle impossible to resolve theoretically or observationally. Of equal importance to Kant, I will argue, is a second question: "how can I be free if there is a God?" In a piece of beautiful economy, Kant's mature answer to both these two questions will be the same. I know Newtonian features of the world because in some sense they are not "out there" in the universe but are features of my reception of the world. And I can be free because the deterministic features of Newtonian physics, which threaten my freedom, are not "out there" in the universe but are features of my reception of the world.

To feel the relief that this answer gives us, we need first of all to work through some of the agony of the problem. To this we now turn. We are still on the first ledge. Having explained to the assembled group that space and time are the products of substances impacting one another, Kant goes on to explain where human freedom fits into the picture. The headline position is that, for Kant in the 1750s, we have no ability to do other than we do, and that we are not ultimately responsible for our actions, but that we are still meaningfully called "free." Let us see how this is supposed to work.

Kant's Early Account of Freedom

Looking up at our created and interconnected universe, we see patterns of causation running from substance to substance. As we have seen, Kant's thought about these patterns is a heady mixture of Leibnizian rationalism and Newtonian physics. From Leibniz he inherits the "principle of sufficient reason," which is to say, the view that for everything that happens there is a full and determining set of reasons and prior causes, such that just this thing had to happen. This works always and everywhere. The particular way in which it manifests itself for Kant has a decidedly Newtonian flavor. Newton's principle of inertia states that "bodies must be externally acted upon for change to occur." Newton's account is restricted to bodies, and forces which have place, direction, and change. Kant applies something like the principle of inertia not just to bodies but also to the fundamental constituents of reality, the created indivisible substances that underlie space and time. Kant states:

> No change can happen to substances except in so far as they are connected with other substances; their reciprocal dependency on each other determines their reciprocal change of state. (*NE,* 1: 410)

A proper Leibnizian, as we have seen, would not accept this claim that fundamental substances are impacted. But Kant does accept this, and sees it as an essential aspect of the Newtonian picture. So where are we in this cosmos? Well, we are created substances among other created substances. As with all other created substances, "no change can happen" except in so far as we are connected with other substances and impacted. This is a principle that goes right down into our very souls, and into the heart of freedom. Human action follows the pattern laid down for all events. Kant writes:

> There is nothing in that which is grounded which was not in the ground itself. For nothing is without a determining ground; accordingly, there is nothing in that which is grounded which does not reveal its determining ground. (*NE,* 1: 406)

This chain of grounding takes us back to God:

> And thus, by tracing one's way along the inexorable chain of events which . . . once and for all snakes its way along and weaves its path through the eternal series of consequences, one eventually arrives at the first state of the world. And this state immediately reveals God, the Creator, the ultimate ground of events, and the fertile ground of so many consequences. Once this ultimate ground is posited, other grounds follow, in accordance with an ever constant law. (*NE,* 1: 399)

> God . . . as Creator, is, so to speak, the well or bubbling spring from which all things flow with infallible necessity down an inclined channel. (*NE,* 1: 403)

Nonetheless, in the 1750s, Kant thinks that we are free. This is only possible because Kant has an unambitious conception of what freedom requires. Freedom does not require the ability to do other than you do, or the status of being ultimately responsible for your actions. All that is required for an action to be free is that you wanted to do something, and that your wanting this arises from who and what you are, rather than being coercively imposed upon you.

Kant's early account of freedom fits into a family of theories of freedom that are called "compatibilist." These theories are called "compatibilist" because our being free is "compatible" with all events in the universe being determined, such that just and only this thing can follow, given the prior state of the universe. According to the early Kant's compatibilist account of freedom, we are free if we do what we want, where we understand what we want, and follow it with our will, even though both our understanding and will are determined by prior states of the universe. These prior states are determined by forces impacting our souls, where these forces snake back ineluctably to an omnipotent God. When weighing up if someone is free, the only relevant question, for the compatibilist, is "did you understand what you were doing, and having understood it, did you want to do this action?" If our subject can answer "yes" in both cases, that is enough to describe the action and the person as "free," warranting the whole industry of ascribing responsibility, praise, and blame to people's free actions.

For the early Kant, as a compatibilist, our free action is determined by impacting forces, and in this respect is no different from a mechanical physical event, or the animal's instinctual behavior. The snooker ball's surface is impacted by the other ball, the dog's instinct is impacted by a scent, and just so the human being's understanding and will are impacted by other created substances. Snooker balls and dogs are not free, even in a compatibilist sense, because they do not have an understanding and a will to be impacted: they do not say, "here is a good that I will." It is what the determining impacting forces hit *upon* that makes all the difference; where they impact an understanding and will, there we have (compatibilist) freedom. As Kant himself puts it, it is the "way in which the certainty of . . . actions is determined by their grounds" which "gives us all the room we need to affirm that they bear the characteristic mark of freedom":

> In the case of brute animals or physico-mechanical actions everything is necessitated in conformity with external stimuli and impulses and without there being any . . . inclination of the will.

We are "free" because

> Human actions are called forth by nothing other than motives of the understanding applied to the will. (*NE*, 1: 403)

All the time, both the understanding and the will are incorporated into the general physics, whereby change can only occur if something is impacted and moved. And such impacts are thoroughly determined. "In the case of the free actions of human beings," Kant writes, because "they are regarded as determinate, their opposites are indeed excluded" (*NE*, 1: 400).

In chapter two, I said that Western philosophy has traditionally considered that there is something more important than "freedom," or something that freedom is ordered toward, and for which freedom is valuable. Different words are given to such a notion, but typically what is envisaged is our achieving our purpose, becoming what we ought to be, flourishing in our properly ordered rational human nature, which leads to harmony, community, and happiness. By the time of his mature thought, Kant will use the term the "highest good" to describe this state. In his early thought, Kant does not use this term, and nor has he fully worked out the concept. Nonetheless, Kant has a strong sense of "perfect freedom," of what it is that rational human nature is for, and a sense that our determined freedom is working well when we stretch out toward our full rationality, and working badly when we turn away from this.

The early Kant is clear that human beings are fully free when they follow the norms of reason, which lead, as a consequence, to happiness and harmony. "Freedom" seems to come in degrees. All one needs for a basic freedom to be operating is that your understanding grasps something, and that you will it. But the more rational you are, the more freedom you enjoy, because your understanding is deeper, and your will more harmonious with these depths. This is so, even though, as we have seen, the depth of our understanding, and the extent of our harmonious willing, are both determined by impacting forces. "Nonetheless, the more certainly it can be said of a person that he submits to the [rational] law," Kant writes, such that "the more that person is determined by all the motives posited for willing," then "the greater is that person's freedom" (*NE*, 1: 402).

I am not going to try to defend the compatibilist account of freedom here. Kant himself becomes unhappy with compatibilism from the 1760s onward, although he cannot initially find a way to free himself from it. This is what really matters to us. In my experience of teaching this material, I find that people tend to have powerful and immoveable prejudices for or against compatibilism. That in itself is interesting, and indicative of the seismic nature of the shift that Kant makes.

The "Unsolvable Metaphysical Difficulty"

The first sign that we get of Kant struggling with his early compatibilism comes in the 1760s, around the time that Kant reads Rousseau. Kant's reflections upon Rousseau are only the first stirrings of an unease that does not fully flower until the 1770s. First of all, I will say something about Rousseau, and then move on to the 1770s.

The only picture hanging in Kant's house was a portrait of Rousseau. There is a well-rehearsed anecdote about Kant's walking habits. Kant would take his evening walk at the same time every day, with his servant Lampe walking behind a few paces carrying the umbrella. On just one day, Kant was late for his walk. On this day, Kant had been reading Rousseau. Rousseau, Kant writes, enjoys the "noble impetus of genius," and Kant declares Rousseau's importance in the moral realm to be equivalent to Newton's in the physical (*Ob*, 2: 219-20).

For our purposes, of tracking the influence of Rousseau upon Kant's account of freedom, we need to know two things about Rousseau's thought. First of all, Rousseau develops the notion of the "general will," whereby a people governs itself rather than being ruled by an external authority. The laws legislated and enacted by a state are construed as the product of this "general will," what everyone would agree upon when reasoning and willing ideally. Second, Rousseau is concerned about the corrupting influences of strands of so-called "civilization," which inculcate competition, vanity, and contorted forms of emotional repression and expression. Human beings have no option, Rousseau recognizes, but to have their natures formed and shaped within a culture. What matters, therefore, is that people are formed and shaped properly. The time to do this is in childhood, and so Rousseau's educational tract *Émile* tracks the ideal education of a child, from the earliest years until young adulthood.

So what is it about Rousseau that makes him the gatekeeper, carrying the keys to the portal that opens onto the second ledge of Kant's purgatory? We might speculate as to whether Rousseau's notion of the "general will" does important work here, where a people governs itself rather than being ruled by an external authority. Perhaps Kant begins to apply a similar instinct to the micro-level, to the human individual. This is an attractive suggestion, worthy of further exploration, but Kant himself does not explicitly put it in these terms. It is easier, from Kant's own observations on Rousseau, to detect the influence of *Émile,* where Rousseau sets out a program of ideal moral education for the young. Rousseau is suspicious of rooting morality in the passions and sentiment, as the passions can enslave the human being. Kant takes from Rousseau a concern that human creatures take their proper place in the created order. This must be neither too high nor too low: "the greatest concern of the human being is to know how he should properly fulfil his station in creation and rightly understand what one must be in order to be a human being" (*Ob,* 2: 216). If the human being "learns gratifications that are above or beneath him," this will "conflict with the arrangements that nature has made for him" and he "will himself disturb the beautiful order of nature and only be ready to damage it":

> He will have left his post . . . since he is not content to be that for which he is destined, where he has left the sphere of a human being he is nothing, and the hole that he has made spreads its own damage to the neighbouring members. (*Ob,* 2: 216)

For this reason the "science that the human being needs" is "that which teaches him properly to fulfil the position that has been assigned to him in the creation, and from which he can learn what one must be in order to be a human being" (*Ob,* 2: 217). When Kant talks of the "proper position" of a human being, he is talking *qua* our being human as such, in relation to God above and to the beasts below, and emphatically not in the "rich man in his castle, poor man at his gate" sense. There is in fact a deeply egalitarian instinct in Kant, as we will see in his aversion to "servitude," which he learns from Rousseau. Kant confesses that before reading Rousseau, he "despised" the "rabble who knows nothing," but that "Rousseau set me right" (*Ob,* 20: 44). As Kant reads Rousseau, he describes how "this blind prejudice vanishes; I learn to respect human nature." Human beings find their proper place in the creation through the exercise of a freedom that tracks morality. Kant writes that obstacles to freedom come in the form of "many external things," including "his concupiscence" and "nature," but that "what is harder and more unnatural than this yoke of necessity is the subjection of one human being under the will of another":

68

No misfortune can be more terrifying to one who is accustomed to freedom, who has enjoyed the good of freedom, than to see himself delivered to a creature of his own kind who can compel him to do what he will (to give himself over to his will). (*Ob,* 2: 230)

The thought of "servitude" is "terrifying," involving a "certain ugliness and a contradiction." It is "absurd and perverse" that a "human being should as it were need no soul himself and have no will of his own," and that "another soul should move my limbs" (*Ob,* 2: 230). Freedom, in that case, would not "elevate me above the cattle," but would "place me beneath them":

Such a person is to himself as it were nothing but the houseware of another. I could just as well indicate my respect to the boots of the master as to his lackey. In short, the person who is dependent in this way is no longer a person, he has lost his rank, he is nothing but a belonging of another person. (*Ob,* 2: 230)

For Kant, even "a small degree of dependency is much too great an evil for it not to be naturally terrifying" (*Ob,* 2: 230). The "greatest perfection" for human beings is "to subordinate everything to the free capacity for choice" (*Ob,* 2: 244-46).

The problem of "subjugation-to-another" has not yet taken its sharpest theological form for Kant. At this stage, Kant distinguishes between subjection to other humans, which is harmful to freedom, and subjection to God, which is not. Although, Kant writes, "the ground of the legislative power presupposes inequality, and causes one person to lose a degree of freedom to another," when the human being is subject to the "divine legislative power" then "he is in accordance with nature" (*Ob,* 2: 222-23).

I want to draw attention to something here. Note Kant's differentiation between dependence upon human beings and dependence upon God, and Kant's initial sense that the latter is not corrosive of freedom in the way that the former is. This instinct takes Kant right back to some premodern theological claims about the relationship between God and human beings (explored further in chapter seven): that God alone, and uniquely, can never be an alien or external cause which threatens the freedom of the creature. Kant moves toward this classical and medieval insight in the early 1760s, but jolts away from it in the 1770s, as I show in the remainder of this chapter.

To appreciate the momentum of Kant's thought here, we can see that it is not hard to frame an initial challenge to the traditional distinction between freedom-damaging inequality between humans on the one hand, and freedom-enhancing inequality between God and the human creature on the other. The challenge would run along the following lines. What matters, in Kant's own words, is that "one must not perform actions from obedience to another person that one could do out of internal motivating grounds" such that it makes us "**slaves**" to "do everything out of obedience where it could have been done from internal motivating grounds" (*Ob*, 2: 222-23). Given that this is what matters, subjugation to the will of God might still seem a form of slavery, indeed, all the more so because of the greater asymmetry between divine and human power. Subjugation does not become less severe because it becomes more total.

In the late 1760s, Kant dramatically, albeit unsystematically, announces a desire to abandon the compatibilist account of freedom that he set out in the 1750s. Kant writes that "freedom consists in the capacity to act independently of external determining grounds in accordance with the intellectual power of choice" (*R* 3872, 17: 319). Kant is now interested in something he calls "absolute spontaneity" or "transcendental freedom," which he insists must be "self-activity from an inner principle according to the power of free choice." Such freedom is an all-or-nothing affair, either "absolute" or "qualified in some respect," and if qualified, no more than the freedom of a "turnspit" (*ML₁*, 28: 269). "Freedom cannot be divided," Kant writes; "the human being is either entirely free or not free at all" (*R* 4229, 17: 467).

We can clearly appreciate the shift in Kant's position when we reflect that in 1755 Kant insisted that our choices are not only "qualified" but entirely determined. In the 1750s, we do indeed enjoy what Kant in the 1770s now calls a "turnspit spontaneity" in relation to the divine designer who creates and sustains us. During the 1770s, the crisis reaches a particularly explicit intensity. Kant just cannot account for how a created being, in relation to God, can be free:

> We can very well understand and have insight into divine freedom, but not human freedom. (*R* 4788, 17: 728)

Kant calls the sort of freedom whereby we can do otherwise, and where we are ultimately responsible for our actions "original causality" or an "original capacity": "original" because we are indeed the origin, the first cause, of our actions. He aligns this with the notion of "efficient causation," that is to say, bringing something into existence, bringing about an effect, and making something happen:

> Freedom is the capacity to produce and effect something originally. But how original causality and an original capacity for efficient causation obtain in a created being is not to be comprehended at all. (*R* 4221, 17: 462)

Between 1776 and 1778 Kant describes this as the "only unsolvable metaphysical difficulty" (*R* 5121, 18: 98), to which he attends at length in his lectures on metaphysics. Some commentators deny that Kant ever moves toward a non-compatibilist conception of freedom, arguing instead that Kant shifts from one type of compatibilism to another.[2] In chapter six, I will say something about such interpretations. We are already in a position to see that, for Kant himself, at least, and whatever terminology we use, there is an important shift in what he wants from freedom, revolving around our ability to "produce and effect something originally," which Kant begins to think requires us to be the "first cause" of our actions.

Conclusion

I am going to draw this chapter to a close by setting out an electrifying passage of Kant's unresolved philosophical anxiety about freedom:

> But it is asked: do the actions of the soul, its thoughts, come from the inner principle which is determined by no causes, or are its actions determined by an external principle? If the latter were [the case], then it would have only spontaneity in some respect, but not without qualification, and thus no freedom in the transcendental sense. If it is assumed ... that the soul has a cause, that it is a dependent being, is an effect of another, then the question here is: whether absolute spontaneity can be attributed to the soul, as a being which has a cause. This is a difficulty which detains us here. Were it an independent being, then we could in any event think in it absolute spontaneity. But if I assume: it is a being derived from another, then it appears to be quite probable that it is

---

2. See Allen W. Wood, "Kant's Compatibilism," in *Self and Nature in Kant's Philosophy*, ed. Allen W. Wood (Ithaca and London: Cornell University Press, 1984), pp. 73-101.

also determined by this cause in all its thoughts and actions, thus has only spontaneity in some respect; that it indeed acts freely according to the inner principle, but is determined by a cause. Now the question is: whether I can think [of myself] as soul? Do I have transcendental spontaneity or absolute freedom? (*ML₁*, 28: 268)

Until the next chapter then, we leave Kant in this state of high agitation and difficulty. "How, given that there is a God, can I be free?," where freedom now requires that we are able to do other than we do, and that we are ultimately responsible for our actions. The problem is that we are making a new demand upon freedom, but standing under the same conceptual planetarium. We still have created substances interconnected by forces, brought into existence and sustained by the divine will selecting from the divine understanding. In the very same lectures where Kant sets out his yearning for "transcendental freedom" or "absolute spontaneity," he again affirms a metaphysics that makes the human possession of such freedom, as he himself puts it, "difficult to comprehend" (*ML₁*, 28: 270). In continuity with his 1750s cosmology, Kant writes that all "necessary universal laws" and the "connection of substances among one another" consist in their constant dependence on the "unity of the primordial being" (*ML₁*, 28: 215), with God being the source of the determining grounds of all events, including the (now problematically) "free" actions of human beings.

Something, somewhere, will have to give. We will see, in the next chapter, that determinism will be sustained, but will become a feature of our reception of the world, rather than being in the world in itself. God will withdraw from some of his traditional creative tasks, and will in some sense cease to be, for Kant, the creator of space and time, and of the determined chains of causation that occur in space and time. We will be able to understand the perplexing claim with which we began this chapter. This was the claim that I do not need to search for the "starry heavens above me" in a "transcendent region beyond my horizon"; rather, we will "see them before me" connected "immediately with the consciousness of my existence" (*CPrR*, 5: 161-62).

We will also see in the next chapter that non-determined human freedom, a freedom that is absolute and "transcendental" (in Kant's terms), will be affirmed, but will remain in a profound sense invisible, but also in some sense connected "immediately with the consciousness of my existence" (*CPrR*, 5: 161-62). Human freedom will be aligned with divine freedom in one sense, but distanced from it in another. The distancing will be as important as the aligning. Like God, we become ultimately responsible for our actions. But unlike God, we will be able to do other than the good. This, Kant thinks, is essential for our moral struggle and flourishing, but nonetheless regrettable: "although the human being . . . can always decide something else," he will write in the 1780s, it is "precisely this which is a lack of freedom in the human being, since he does *not always* act according to his reason," whereas it is "true freedom in God that he decides only what is in conformity with his highest understanding" (*LPR,* 28: 1068).

This might provoke us to ask whether the whole fight for human freedom in relation to God was worth the candle after all, if what we have won is, as Kant puts it in another text, "a loss," leading him to reflect that the "history" of human freedom "begins with evil" (*CHH,* 8: 107-23), represented mythologically (for Kant) by the original and incomprehensible bad choice in Eden.

This chapter has set out the problem. The next two chapters set out Kant's solution, but also some problems with the solution. Chapters seven and eight examine some problems with the problem.

CHAPTER FIVE

Creating Freedom: Kant's Theological Solution

In the previous chapter, we left Kant stumbling through the darkness and the fog, unable to account for how we can be meaningfully free, given that we are created by God. This is the theological problem that besets Kant in the 1760s and 1770s. We saw that Kant's problem emerges from a world-view that is a complex interweaving of rationalist and Newtonian strands of thought. From rationalism, mediated through Leibniz, Kant inherits assumptions about the fundamental layer of reality, beyond and behind the realm of appearances. At this fundamental level, behind the "phenomenal" realm (which means "that which appears"), substances are instantiations of the essences that are part of the divine understanding; as such they are indivisible, non-spatial, and non-temporal. Many of the rationalists whom we met in the previous chapter, on the second ledge of Kant's purgatory, are also convinced that these fundamental substances cannot be impacted by other substances. Kant does not agree, and a distinctive commitment of his early thought is that these created substances are impacted by other created substances. This is how change occurs. Space and time are the products of the forces of attraction and repulsion between these created substances. These chains of causation, produced by the forces that run between substances, are entirely deterministic: one thing follows another along unswerving iron rails. At the source of all these chains of causation is the creator, God.

Such a cosmology is unproblematic as long as Kant thinks that our freedom does not require that we are able to do otherwise, or that we are ultimately responsible for our actions. We saw in the previous chapter how Kant's views on freedom shifted in the 1760s and 1770s, perhaps in part through the provocation of reading Rousseau. Kant begins to require of human freedom that we be able to do other than we do, and that we be ultimately responsible for our actions. I indicated that something in Kant's worldview would have to give. Now it is time to watch the collapse.

In outline, this is how it will work. What is the source of the problem for our freedom? The problem is God, and God's creation of space and time, and then of us, subject as we are to the forces that make up space and time. Space and time, Kant is convinced, are irretrievably, intrinsically, obviously contaminated with, and saturated in, determinism. The commitment that collapses is the claim that God is the creator of space and time. We, that is, human beings, become in some sense the creators of space and time. Space and time cease to be the products of the interconnection between created substances, and become instead the products of the way in which we encounter other created substances. As such, space and time, and all the consequent determinism, become relativized, as features of our experience of the world, of how the world appears to us, rather than being in the world independently of us. They become, properly speaking, "mere phenomena," merely the way the world appears *to us,* and not the way the world is. As Kant himself puts it:

> Thus space is nothing in itself and is not a thing as a divine work, but rather lies in us and can only obtain in us. (*R* 6057, 18: 439)

Space and time are the source of the determinism that obstructs Kant's more ambitious conception of freedom. But if space and time are features not of the world, but of our reception of the world, then we do not come downstream of space and time. We are not constrained by, and subject to, spatial and temporal determinism.

This gives rise to a sharp question: how does Kant justify such a shift? What is his evidence? What is his theoretical warrant? It is here that the real beauty and elegance of Kant's "critical shift" becomes apparent, and we see something of the harmonious and systematic nature of his thought. In the first part of this chapter, I will show how Kant only arrives at his solution to the problem of our created freedom by pushing hard on the question of evidence and knowledge, and then pushing again. Here we see an example of Kant's strong ethic governing belief formation, where he is prepared to overturn everything, while trying not to give up anything of importance. The solution that space and time are features of our reception of the world, rather than being in the world in itself, we will see, is good news both for knowledge and for freedom. The solution is required to

75

protect knowledge, to show discipline in forming beliefs, and to preserve freedom.

In the previous chapter, we climbed two ledges of purgatory with Kant, our Virgil. On the first ledge, we found rationalists telling tales around the campfire, explaining how their non-spatial and non-temporal fundamental substances manage to generate the appearance of a Newtonian universe. On the second ledge, Kant stumbles over the question of our freedom. Before spiraling around the mountain to Kant's solution, which he will arrive at by deepening some of the lessons learned on the first ledge, we need to go through more darkness and confusion, climbing with Kant onto the third ledge, where he is gripped with further doubts, not only about freedom, but also about our knowledge.

Metaphysical Dreams

On the third ledge we find an aristocratic gentleman, Baron von Swedenborg. The Baron is sitting at an empty dinner table, made up elaborately for twenty or so, complete with beautiful silver centerpieces and cut crystal. In every respect Swedenborg appears, in Kant's own words (where Kant is quoting a trusted friend), "intelligent, gracious and open-hearted . . . a scholar" (*Corr,* 10: 45). Except that he is talking, laughing, listening, nodding, reprimanding, all animatedly into the empty air, as if all the empty chairs are occupied by the most engaging and talkative of guests. Swedenborg is talking to the citizens of the spirit world: he claims to be able to communicate widely with the spirit world, with those who have departed from any point in history, or from any part of the world.

We will do well here to remember the rooms that we explored, before setting out on our journey with Kant. In the mid-1780s, we found ourselves in the same rationalist hall that we had visited in the 1760s, except that the room was more stripped-back, more subtle, more tasteful. There were also a few additions to the room: a miniature of David Hume on the writing desk (which I will address shortly), but also some hefty tomes hidden under a cushion. These tomes were authored by the same mystic Baron whom we meet now, the Swedish aristocrat who claims to be well connected with the spirit world. We made a note to ask Kant about this later on in the journey. Now is the time to make good on this intention.

If we had leafed through Kant's copies of Swedenborg's volumes, we might have come across drafts of letters written by Kant. From around 1762 or 1763 (the date is a little smudged) we find a letter addressed to Charlotte von Knobloch. Kant recounts various extraordinary stories regarding the Baron. In a charming mixture of the occult, the chivalrous, and the domestic, Swedenborg saves a widow from extortion: her lately departed husband informs Swedenborg where a receipt can be found, which proves that a costly silver service has been paid for. In another anecdote, which became widely famous and believed, the Baron leaves a dinner party in Gothenburg, hosted, and so witnessed, by the Queen of Sweden, ambassadors, and professors. Swedenborg is highly agitated because of a fire many miles away in Stockholm, which he knows to have just started. By report, Swedenborg describes in great detail, simultaneously with the unfolding events, the cause of the fire, its progress, and then its dying down. Not until two days later does news of the fire reach Gothenburg. Swedenborg, it turns out, was correct in every detail. Kant's remarks on this anecdote are striking: the event, he writes, "seems to me to have the greatest weight . . . and really removes any conceivable doubt" (*Corr*, 10: 46). In the same letter Kant writes: "I eagerly await the book Swedenborg intends to publish" (*Corr*, 10: 48).

Kant goes on to buy, and to read, all the volumes of Swedenborg's *Arcana Coelesti* ("Secrets of the Heavens"). Doing so has the impact of a small earthquake on Kant's self-confidence. We see the quake under way in the most bizarre and tortured of Kant's works, his 1766 text *Dreams of a Spirit-Seer,* where he engages with Swedenborg's visions and adventures. Kant does not like the books. His dislike is expressed at two levels. At the more superficial level, he considers that they are, as he puts it, "stuffed full of nonsense," with not a "single drop of reason" to be found in them (*D,* 2: 360). Kant "confesses, with a certain humiliation, to having been naive enough to investigate the truth of some of the stories" (*D,* 2: 318). Kant finds, as he puts it, "what one usually finds when one has no business searching at all, exactly nothing!" (*D,* 2: 318). Kant laments that he "went to the expense of purchasing a lengthy work, and, what was worse . . . to the trouble of reading it as well" (*D,* 2: 318). Quoting "the sharp-sighted *Hudibras,*" a satire by Samuel Butler, Kant diagnoses Swedenborg's condition: "*if a . . . wind should rage in the guts, what matters is the direction it takes: if downwards, then the result is a fart; if upwards, an apparition or an heavenly inspiration*" (*D,* 2: 348).

So Swedenborg's works are full of nonsense. But what Kant *really* does not like, I would argue, what really shakes Kant, is this: Swedenborg has held up a mirror, in which Kant is horrified to find his own reflection. Once stripped of all his adventures, what is it that Swedenborg actually claims to survey, while piloting what Kant calls his "airship of metaphysics" (*D*, 2: 360)? In the first part of the *Dreams of a Spirit-Seer*, Kant offers a sort of philosophical reconstruction of the metaphysics that underlies Swedenborg's account. Swedenborg claims to have access to a world inhabited by non-spatial and non-temporal substances that underlie appearances. These substances, or "spirits," somehow, as Kant himself puts it, fill space not by occupying space, but by means of an "active force (of repulsion)" (*D*, 2: 323). The substances, or spirits, themselves are not "extended" in space, but "only occupy a space in virtue of the *external* effect they produce on other substances" (*D*, 2: 323-24).

Now, where have we heard this sort of thing before? I would suggest, in the previous chapter, sitting around the purgatorial fire of the rationalists. Remember the rationalists seizing in turn the silver spheres that represented the fundamental non-spatial and non-temporal substances that constitute reality, and each of them attempting their own account of how these fundamental realities relate to the Newtonian phenomena of our everyday life and of observational science? Swedenborg has drunk deeply of his "moon-flasks" (*D*, 2: 360), as Kant puts it, and his mind gives birth to "mooncalves." But, what, fundamentally is so different about Swedenborg's dreams, the dreams of a spirit-seer, and the dreams of metaphysicians such as Leibniz, Wolff, Baumgarten, and Kant? Do they not all, in different ways and with different results (in itself indicative of a problem), claim some sort of knowledge of non-spatial and non-temporal substances that underlie what can be observed? Leibniz and others do not ask these substances about missing receipts, but what ultimately is the difference between Swedenborg's "nonsense" and the metaphysics of Leibniz and Kant?

This, at any rate, is Kant's question. Quoting Aristotle, Kant writes that *"when we are awake we share a common world, but when we dream each has a world of his own"* (*D*, 2: 342). Kant reverses this, to derive the following principle: "if different people have each of them their own world, then we may suppose that they are dreaming" (*D*, 2: 342). Kant then describes philosophers such as Wolff and Crusius as *"those who build castles in the sky in their various imaginary worlds"* (*D*, 2: 342). Although these "dreamers of reason" do not experience apparitions in the manner of Swedenborg, Kant writes that they are no different in the following respect: "they see something which no other normal person sees; they have their own community with beings which reveal themselves to no one else, no matter how good his senses may be" (*D*, 2: 342). Kant is clear about how his own thought is implicated. He writes, "I find myself in the following unfortunate predicament," as Swedenborg's "testimony" which "looks so desperately deformed and foolish," bears an "uncommon likeness" to the "philosophical figment of my imagination" (*D*, 2: 359), which Kant now calls disparagingly "my own pretentious theory of the community of spirits" (*D*, 2: 349). Reflecting on the "seductive comparisons" that can be drawn between his own thought and that of the flatulent Baron, Kant tells us "without beating about the bush": "I have no sense of humour" (*D*, 2: 359).

It is more usual to identify David Hume as the principal catalyst for Kant's turn away from traditional metaphysics. Kant himself seems to warrant this, when he writes in 1783 that it was the "remembrance of David Hume" that woke him from his "dogmatic slumber" (*Pr*, 4: 260). In terms of texts that Kant produces at the time, when he is actually emerging from his "dogmatic slumber," it is in fact Swedenborg who demonstrably gets under Kant's skin. This is consistent with Kant blushing at the remembrance of Hume. Kant imagines himself sitting at Swedenborg's table, while being observed by a figure such as Hume, who always pushes the question of evidence and justification. It could have been the "remembrance" of Hume that particularly shames Kant, as he finds himself associated, in the forum of his own conscience, with Swedenborg. There is another, perhaps less generous, explanation for Kant acknowledging Hume, rather than the Baron. We can perhaps understand why Kant would prefer to credit a figure of the stature of Hume, rather than explaining that he had spent much of his early forties filling his head with the lunar Baron, with whom he was not amused to find that he had much in common. In any case, when reading Kant's acknowledgment to Hume, we must always read the next sentence, which is often omitted. Kant explains that he was provoked by Hume's insight into a "part of" the *problem* of how we have knowledge of causation, while insisting at the same time that he was "very far from listening to [Hume] with respect to his conclusions" (*Pr*, 4: 260). This, we will find, is absolutely correct. Kant will eventually answer the skeptical problems, posed, in very different ways, by Hume and Swedenborg, by digging deeper into Platonic strands in his rationalist legacy.

In *Dreams of a Spirit-Seer*, we have a tipping-point in Kant's philosophy. It expresses some of the most skeptical anxieties in the whole of Kant's thought, alongside a continuing, if painful, devotion to metaphysics. If Kant had been taken from the world in 1767, it might have remained forever unclear which way the scales would have finally tipped: toward a despondent skepticism, or toward some sort of resolution and solidification of the grounds of a non-flatulent metaphysics. By "skepticism" here, I mean an inability to form beliefs, because of a crisis of confidence in the justification for these beliefs. In fact, Kant lives on, skepticism is defeated, and metaphysics is put on a more modest but firmer footing.

Even if skepticism *had* triumphed, which it did not, then we can be clear that Kant would have been despondent and depressed at this result. In *Dreams of a Spirit-Seer* Kant writes repeatedly, longingly, almost poetically of his metaphysical hopes. As a literary device, I have been describing Kant as our Virgil. In *Dreams of a Spirit-Seer,* Kant provides some warrant for this, explicitly quoting Virgil's epic poem the *Aeneid.* The poem recounts the journey of Aeneas, from his destroyed home city of Troy, sacked by the Greeks, to Italy, where Aeneas founds a people who will become the Romans.

Early on in the *Aeneid,* when Troy is sacked, Aeneas loses his wife Creusa. In rage and despair he searches for her, and is met by her departed shade, who instructs him to abandon Troy. Aeneas reaches out to Creusa, attempting in vain to clasp her shade. Kant quotes Aeneas's description of his attempt to embrace the image of his dead wife:

> Three times I tried to put my arms around her neck. Three times her phantom melted in my arms, as weightless as the wind, as light as the flight of sleep. (*D,* 2: 367; *Aeneid,* II: 790-91)

There can be no doubt about the identity of Kant's lost beloved, whose shadow and image he tries in vain to embrace. Kant tells us: it is "metaphysics," "with which, as fate would have it, I have fallen in love" (*D,* 2: 367). As Virgil describes Creusa, so Kant could describe his beloved: "she faded into insubstantial air, leaving me there in tears" (*Aeneid,* II: 790-91).

At a mid-point in Virgil's narrative, the hero Aeneas descends into the Underworld, the "realm of shades" (*D,* 2: 317). In *Dreams of a Spirit-Seer,* Kant quotes Virgil's description of Aeneas's descent:

> They walked in the darkness of that lonely night with shadows all about them, through the empty halls of Dis and his desolate kingdom. (*D,* 2: 329; *Aeneid,* VI: 268-69)

"Let it be right for me to tell what I have been told," Kant quotes (*D,* 2: 340; *Aeneid,* VI: 267-68). And if we follow the passage in Virgil, we find:

"let it be with your divine blessing that I reveal what is hidden deep in the mists beneath the earth" (*Aeneid,* VI: 267-68). What are those things that are hidden? They are shadows and desolation.

In Virgil's second incarnation, in Dante's *Purgatory,* he must warn off his devoted admirer and fellow-poet Statius from bending the knee to him:

> But Virgil said: "No brother. Shade you are,
> and shade am I. You must not kneel to me."
> . . .
> "Forgetting we are empty semblances
> and taking shadows to be substances."
>
> (Dante, *Purgatorio,* Canto XXI, lines 130-37)

We can hardly ask for a better description of the desolation that Swedenborg produces in Kant, the anxiety that he has been taking "shadows to be substances." We have spent long enough with the lunar Baron, and leaving him to his shadowy dinner party, we need to know how Kant is able to move out of Swedenborg's reach, and to disentangle himself from the Baron's extravagant knowledge claims about a world of shadows, without capitulating to skepticism.

The Year of Great Light

Kant turns forty in 1764. He announces this to be a significant event. According to Kant's psychological theory, we only reach maturity in the fortieth year, and only then are we able really to undertake the systematic attempt "to become a better human being" (*APV,* 7: 201, 294). Within a few years, Kant might have considered this to be too optimistic an assessment, as in his early forties, we can see that Kant has managed to cook up for himself an impressive mid-life crisis: he wants to be free, but cannot find a way, and he fears he must leave his beloved metaphysics. Or, slightly more formally, "how, given that we are created by God, can we be free?" And how, given that all we experience are appearances, can we claim to know anything secure about underlying or fundamental reality? We are now ready to see unraveled the elegance of Kant's single mature solution to both crisis points. In 1769 Kant has what he describes as a "year of great light." What is it that Kant discovers in 1769, except perhaps that we achieve maturity not at forty, but at forty-five?

It is, in his words, that *"space is not something objective and real . . .* it issues from the nature of the mind in accordance with a stable law . . . so to speak, for co-ordinating everything which is sensed externally" (*ID*, 2: 403). As it is for space, so it goes for time: time issues from the nature of our minds, from the way in which we receive the world. Space and time are not features of the world as it is in itself. They are features of our reception of the world. This is hugely significant for the nature of causation, because causation, for us, is intrinsically spatial and temporal. Causation happens in space and time. This means that spatio-temporal causation is also not a feature of the world in itself, but rather of our reception of the world.

This is good news for both knowledge and freedom. I will explain how this works for both, respectively. First of all, I will set out how knowledge is preserved. Kant wants, among other things, to ground our knowledge of the physical universe, which he considers to be explicable in terms of Newtonian forces. In his thought before the "year of great light," Kant considered that space and time were the products of forces of attraction and repulsion between (non-spatial and non-temporal) substances. Swedenborg and Hume between them undermined Kant's confidence in this account: how can he know that non-spatial and non-temporal substances interact in such a way to produce Newtonian space and time? But if space and time, and everything therein, are features not of an inaccessible world "out there" but rather features of our reception of the world, then there is nothing about them that we cannot know. We know space and time, and about spatio-temporal causation, because in some sense they are products of our minds, features of our reception of the world. In Kant's own words, our knowledge of the Euclidean structure of space and time is akin to the way in which the geometer knows the properties of a triangle, having constructed the triangle himself:

> He had to ascribe to the thing nothing except what followed necessarily from what he himself had put into it in accordance with its concept. (B xii)

Now we are able to understand the perplexing quotation with which we began the previous chapter, the passage from the second *Critique*, quoted on Kant's tombstone. This was the claim that I do not need to search for the "starry heavens above me" in a "transcendent region beyond my horizon," but that we will "see them before me" connected "immediately with the consciousness of my existence" (*CPrR*, 5: 161-62). The starry heavens, all the "countless multitude of worlds" that can seem to annihilate my significance, are like all appearances in space and time: in their vast spatiality and temporality, they are features of my reception of the world, and not in a "transcendent region beyond my horizon." When I see the starry heavens, I am indeed connected "immediately with the consciousness of my existence."

We know that in the 1760s Kant studied a *History of Philosophy* written by Johann Formey, where he would have read about Plato's distinction between that which underlies reality, the intelligible forms, and that which appears. In 1770, when Kant announces his discovery about the status of space and time, he explicitly draws on Platonic language of noumena and phenomena (that which underlies experience, and that which appears), and cites Plato approvingly (*ID*, 2: 396, 413). It is possible to understand Kant's solution to his crisis of knowledge as an intensification of certain Platonic strands in rationalism, enriched and made more fundamental by reflecting on the source of this tradition, Plato himself. What we see happening in rationalism as mediated to Kant through Leibniz, Wolff, and Baumgarten, is this: we have a fairly direct relationship between the underlying substances and the Newtonian appearances or effects of these substances. Both Leibniz and Wolff, for example, think that knowledge of underlying reality, and of that which appears, is somehow on the same spectrum. When we know something as it appears, we have a "confused" perception of the thing itself. For example, Wolff argues that space is a "confused" perception of fundamental properties of substances. Plato himself would find this variant of Platonism too thin, with too much access to the world of forms, of fundamental reality. For Plato, although everything that appears depends on what is fundamentally real, it does not do so in such a way that we can, even confusedly, know the underlying reality, or at least not in this bodily life.

I have used the term "Platonism" a few times now in my discussion, and will do so more. I want to reflect here a little on the warrant for doing so. The invocation of Platonism might jar in the context of Kant, especially if the primary association of Platonism is what seems an extravagant and speculative invocation of a mysterious world of forms, inaccessible and invisible, with a fundamentally dualistic picture distinguishing a world that appears from this world of intelligible forms. These associations are unfair to both Plato and Kant, and are not intended here. It is important, then, for me to say what is intended. In the recent literature on Plato and Platonism, there are three predominant accounts of how the category of "Platonism"

should be construed. These could be described as the textual, the conceptual, and the existential. My claim will be that on all three accounts, there is warrant for considering strands of Kant's thought to be "Platonic." A textual construal insists that there must be some explicit commentary on the texts or ideas of Plato himself.[1] The conceptual construal, set out by Lloyd P. Gerson,[2] characterizes Platonism as a shared constellation of philosophical assumptions, including the following:

- The universe has a systematic unity, which is reflected in our understanding, which ties together metaphysics, epistemology, ethics, and aesthetics.
- The simple precedes the complex.
- The more perfect precedes the less perfect.
- The intelligible (that which underlies appearances) precedes the sensible and empirical.
- The category of the divine has far-reaching explanatory power at a fundamental level.
- The intellectual is not derived from the physical, but is prior to it.
- There are degrees of perfection and of insight.
- Moral and aesthetic qualities are woven into reality, and degrees of moral and aesthetic insight are possible.
- Human fulfillment involves a restoration of something lost, and involves a deepening participation in a structure of reason that transcends the individual.
- Inasmuch as divinity and reason are identified, human fulfillment is described in terms of the classical Platonic exhortation to "become like god."

As significant as what is present in this list, is what is missing: there is no mention of a theory of a "world of forms" or of a dualism between appearances and this world of forms. In the *Parmenides* Plato himself offers a powerful critique of the theory of forms, and a dualistic model, as I will show in the next chapter, hardly captures the subtlety of Platonic or Kantian

1. This approach is represented in a number of works by Douglas N. Sedley, in particular "Plato's *Auctoritas* and the Rebirth of the Commentary Tradition," in *Philosophia Togata II: Plato and Aristotle at Rome,* ed. Jonathan Barnes and Miriam Griffin (Oxford: Clarendon Press, 1997).

2. Lloyd P. Gerson in *Aristotle and Other Platonists* (Ithaca, NY: Cornell University Press, 2005).

patterns of thought, which are more about a textured unveiling of ultimate
reality than a dichotomy between appearances and an intelligible realm.

The existential construal of Platonism, set forward by Pierre Hadot,[3]
emphasizes the practical dimension of Platonism. Hadot explains that Platonism, like other classical schools, was a "way of life," which is not ex-
hausted by explicit philosophical discourse or argumentation. The Platonic
way of life involved a death to the self and individuality by a participation in
reason itself. In the process of Socratic dialogue, we question ourselves and
transcend our individuality, rising to the level of universality. The point of
the study of geometry and mathematics is, for example, to purify the mind
from sensible representations, with an explicitly ethical end in sight, found
in self-transcending agreement with others who also participate in reason.
Intrinsic to dialogue and reason is an "ethics of self-transcendence." Explicit
"spiritual exercises" are oriented to this purpose, including exercises where
we prepare for sleep, as an echo of preparing for death; in both sleep and
death, there is an overcoming of the individual self. The exercise of reason
is conceived of as akin to a type of death, in that the corporeal individual
ceases to exist, or to be limited to that existence, when it transcends itself by
participating in reason. In a process of *askesis,* we purify the intelligence by
divesting it of the passions. Although ostensibly an interior and "individual"
pursuit, the aspiration is to transcend self and join a community of reason,
in a harmony with other selves, but also with the whole cosmos.

Although the textual, conceptual, and existential construals are sometimes treated as competing alternatives, I consider that all of these accounts capture valuable and insightful aspects. Significantly, the category
of Platonism can be applied to Kant on all three accounts. That is to say,
in Kant there are (i) explicit and approving textual references to Plato,
(ii) Platonic philosophical commitments (as identified by Gerson), along
with (iii) Platonic implications for how to live (as identified by Hadot).
I will address the third construal in chapter eight. The second is richly
demonstrated throughout this book. In chapters two and three, we saw
Kant's aspiration to systematicity, undergirded by his conception of the
fundamental unity and harmony of reason, and of reality, with degrees of
insight and perfection. We saw how the more perfect precedes the less,
and the simple precedes the complex, with the divine having far-reaching
explanatory power, albeit that we require practical reason fully to unlock

3. Pierre Hadot's *What Is Ancient Philosophy?* (Cambridge, MA: Harvard University
Press, 2002).

this explanatory power. Practical reason has this power, because moral and aesthetic qualities are, we must believe, woven into reality. The salience to Kant of descriptions on Gerson's list will be amply demonstrated in what remains of this book: that the intelligible (that which underlies appearances) precedes the sensible and empirical (addressed in this chapter), and that human fulfillment involves a restoration of something lost, and involves a deepening participation in a structure of reason that transcends the individual (discussed in chapter eight). In chapter eight, we will even see how Kant finds his way to the Platonic exhortation to "become like god," precisely insofar as divinity and reason are identified.

Finally, Kant includes explicit and approving discussion of Plato. This approval is qualified, and readers have tended to focus on the qualification. But the approval comes first, and is striking. We have already seen in chapter three that Kant endorses a classical conception of philosophy as the search for wisdom. Kant offers detailed praise for Plato in the first *Critique,* writing that "Plato found his ideas preeminently in everything that is practical, i.e., in what rests on freedom, which for its part stands under cognitions that are a proper product of reason" (A 314-15/B 271-72). In the sphere of moral reflection, Kant considers that Plato is correct not "to draw the concepts of virtue from experience," as this would "at best serve as an example for imperfect illustration," when in fact, "we are all aware that when someone is represented as a model of virtue"

> We always have the true original in our own mind alone, with which we compare this alleged model and according to which alone we estimate it. But it is this that is the idea of virtue, in regard to which all possible objects of experience do service as examples (proofs of the feasibility, to a certain degree, of what the concept of reason requires), but never as archetypes. That no human being will ever act adequately to what the pure idea of virtue contains does not prove in the least that there is something chimerical in this thought. For it is only by means of this idea that any judgement of moral worth or unworth is possible; and so it necessarily lies at the ground of every approach to moral perfection, even though the obstacles in human nature, as yet to be determined as to their degree, may hold us at a distance from it. (A 314-15/B 271-72)

As we would expect, the route to Plato's insight is practical reason. As we saw in chapter three, once practical reason finds warrant for such an assertion, there are ramifications and resonances for theoretical reason.

And so it is here, as Kant follows his account of Plato and practical reason with a surprising extension of his approval:

> But Plato was right to see clear proofs of an origin in ideas not only where human reason shows true causality, and where ideas become efficient causes (of actions and their objects), namely in morality, but also in regard to nature itself. A plant, an animal, the regular arrangement of the world's structure (presumably thus also the whole order of nature) — these show clearly that they are possible only according to ideas; although no individual creature, under the individual conditions of its existence, is congruent with the idea of what is most perfect of its species (as little as a human being is congruent with the idea of humanity that he bears in his soul as the archetype of his actions), nevertheless these ideas are in the highest understanding individual, unalterable, thoroughly determined, and the original causes of things, and only the whole of its combination in the totality of a world is fully adequate to its idea. (A 317-18/B 374-75)

Kant does qualify his support for Plato, precisely in the way we would expect. Kant explains that when Plato extends his "concept to speculative cognitions," and claims knowledge of the world of forms (if he does)

> I cannot follow him in this, just as little as I can in the mystical deduction of these ideas or in the exaggerated way in which he hypostatized them, as it were. (A 314/B 371)

Even here, though, the qualification of Kant's support for Plato is itself qualified, in that Kant reflects that "the lofty language that served [Plato] in this field is surely quite susceptible of a milder interpretation, and one that accords better with the nature of things" (A 314/B 371). Kant explains that

> If we abstract its exaggerated expression, then the philosopher's [Plato's] spiritual flight, which considers the physical copies in the world order, and then ascends to their architectonic connection according to ends, i.e., ideas, is an endeavor that deserves respect and imitation. (A 318/B 375)

So, "Plato is right," Kant says, to ground order in underlying ideas and archetypes, albeit by extending something that is warranted by our commitment to freedom and morality. Furthermore, the "ascent" from "physical copies in the world order" to an "architectonic connection, according to ends, i.e., ideas," is an "endeavor that deserves respect and imitation," as long as we strip away "exaggerated expressions" of this project, and avoid "speculative cognitions." Kant's mature critical thought, Kant himself seems to intimate, is an epistemically disciplined and chastened variation on a Platonic theme.

Before his intellectual crisis, Kant shared in the rationalist tendency to move fairly rapidly to underlying reality: so Kant claimed that space and time are direct products of the interaction between fundamental substances. When Kant solves his intellectual crisis, he does so by pushing harder and deeper on the Platonism in rationalism, where Kant himself has told us that Plato's ascent to the intelligible "deserves respect and imitation." Kant himself shows such respect, and attempts an imitation, while attempting to avoid the mistakes made by Plato, or by his readers. After "the year of great light" Kant tells us that appearances are mere representations of how things are, and are not even confused cognitions of things in themselves. Although the appearance depends upon the thing in itself, it does not resemble or disclose the nature of the thing in itself. "All appearances," Kant tells us "are mere representations and not things in themselves," and so "time and space" are only "forms of our intuition," that is, ways in which we receive the world, "but not conditions of objects as things in themselves" (A 369). Only if this is the case, Kant is convinced, can we have knowledge about space and time. Kant writes that if space and time were "something given in themselves (independently of our sensibility)" (A 369), they would be shrouded in mystery.

Knowledge is restricted to that which appears, which Kant calls variously the "phenomenal" or "empirical" realm. It is possible that reality as it underlies what appears (which Kant calls "intelligible" or "noumenal" reality) is radically different from that which appears. What sort of access can we have to reality as it underlies appearance? Certainly we never have knowledge, or at least, never knowledge beyond the minimal awareness that what we experience is merely a representation of something more fundamental. We know, or we must postulate in order to ground the knowledge that we do have, that there are things-in-themselves, which fundamentally ground appearances. What these things-in-themselves are like, what real possibilities govern their existence, and how they interact, and how they ground the world of appearances: about all these things we must learn to say, "I do not know." Herein lies Kant's mature "discipline" in forming beliefs, the shift away from unsubstantiated knowledge claims. We cannot know that we are free or not according to theoretical reason.

It might look as if Kant has so closed down what we can know, that a sort of skepticism has in fact triumphed: about the world in itself, we know nothing. To understand that skepticism has not triumphed, we need to go back to something discussed in the third chapter: the different textures of ways in which we can form beliefs about things. *Knowing* about things is only one way in which we form true beliefs, and, for the mature Kant, perhaps not the most important way. Many of our *true* beliefs are formed through practical reason, which is ordered, we recall, to the good: to that which ought to be done. Kant considers that, as limited human creatures, we are not so very good at knowing about things, especially things in themselves, independently of our spatial and temporal way of receiving them; but as rational believing creatures, we fairly excel, understanding well which beliefs are required in order to support a life dedicated to seeking the good.

Kant, we recall, arrived at rationally warranted (and required) belief in a rationalist God, on the basis that it ought to be the case that being moral leads to happiness, where only God could guarantee this happiness. He also uses practical reason to arrive at his conviction that we are genuinely free. Kant writes that if morality is to be possible, we must postulate that we are free:

> Morality is that which, if it is correct, positively presupposes freedom. If the former is true, then freedom is proved. (A 558/B 586; E CLXXVI; 23: 42)

Recall, from chapter three, that where practical reason sees that a certain set of beliefs is required in order to achieve a good, then we are warranted, indeed required, to hold those beliefs, on the basis of practical reason, as long as what we believe is not known to be impossible. If theoretical reason "had proved that freedom cannot be thought at all," Kant acknowledges, then "freedom and with it morality" would "have to give way to the mechanism of nature" (B xxvii-xxix). But theoretical reason has *not* proved that freedom is impossible, because we know that the way in which things appear is not the same as the way things fundamentally are. Kant is clear about the inextricable link between his new humility about what we can know, mere appearances, and the conceptual space for genuine freedom. He writes:

> For if appearances are things in themselves, then freedom cannot be saved. Then nature is the completely determining cause, sufficient in itself, of every occurrence. (A 536/B 564)

In the second *Critique* Kant asserts that "regarding space and time as determinations belonging to the existence of things" would also lead to a "fatalism of actions" (*CPrR*, 5: 102), where the "last and highest" source of the "long series" of "determining causes" is "found entirely in an alien hand" (*CPrR*, 5: 101), that is, in God, who would be conceived as initiating deterministic chains of cause and effect. Kant is now able to affirm instead that God does not create us within space and time, but that God creates us as, in some sense, the source of space and time, in that space and time are features of our reception of the world. We do not come downstream of deterministic space and time; but deterministic space and time comes downstream of us. The way in which Kant insists upon this is very striking. He says explicitly in the second *Critique* that God must not be regarded as the creator of space and time, and therefore of appearances (which are spatial and temporal):

> Just as it would be a contradiction to say that God is the creator of appearances, so it is also a contradiction to say that as creator he is the cause of actions in the sensible world and thus of actions as appearances, even though he is the cause of the existence of the acting beings (as noumena). (*CPrR*, 5: 102)

In as much as our empirical selves are appearances, we must also say that God is not the creator of our phenomenal selves. God is indeed the creator of noumenal reality, and so of us, as we fundamentally are. Just before the passage cited above, Kant underlines this, writing that "*God as universal original being is the cause of the existence of substances*" (*CPrR*, 5: 100), where "substances" here indicate noumenal substances in distinction to the phenomenal appearance of these substances. Nonetheless, with respect to our spatial and temporal existence, Kant insists, it no longer makes "the slightest difference that the acting beings are creatures" (*CPrR*, 5: 102). Our status as creatures "has to do with [our] intelligible but not [our] sensible existence and therefore cannot be regarded as the determining ground of appearances" (*CPrR*, 5: 102).

The quotation given at the beginning of the chapter ("space . . . is not a thing as a divine work") can now be placed in a larger context, and should now make more sense:

Whatever God did is good, but it does not lie in the sensible world [which is] a mere schema [appearance, mediated through space and time] of the intelligible world. Thus space is nothing in itself and is not a thing as a divine work, but rather lies in us and can only obtain in us. . . . The appearances are not actually creations, thus neither is the human being; rather he is merely the appearance of a divine creation. His condition of acting and being acted upon is an appearance and depends on him as bodies depend on space. The human being is the *principium originarium* [originating principle] of appearances. (*R* 6057, 18: 439)

In my experience, some Kant scholars are liable to be skeptical of the suggestion that space and time, for Kant, are not directly created by God. What has to be insisted upon, in response to this skepticism, is that this is what Kant says, in a number of places. Our task as interpreters is to understand what Kant might possibly mean by this, not to doubt that he said such a thing because we do not know what it means. Part of the meaning, as we see here, is that Kant wishes to make space and time less fundamental aspects of the created realm, coming downstream not of God's direct creative act, but instead downstream of our reception of the world. To be sure, we are still created and sustained by God, and to that extent, God supports our reception of the world in spatial and temporal terms, but only indirectly. What precisely this "indirect" support amounts to will be the subject of chapter seven.

What matters for our purposes here is that the appearance of things as determined is not the same as reality in itself being determined. Kant even goes as far as saying that we achieve a certain "knowledge" *(Wissen)* about our freedom, albeit a knowledge achieved on practical rather than theoretical grounds (*CPrR,* 5: 4; see also *CPrR,* 5: 105). Theoretical reason, we recall, is our reason oriented toward the truth, practical reason toward what one ought to be.

This "knowledge" (achieved on practical grounds) can help us to close one of the interpretative gaps in Kant's system: why Kant seems to be *convinced* that things-in-themselves are not determined, and so, among other things, not spatial or temporal. A standard question is this: how can Kant know this, if the noumenal world of things-in-themselves is indeed unknowable? The objection is often called the "neglected alternative" problem, where the alternative that is thought to be neglected is the possibility that things-in-themselves, for all we know, might be deterministic, and might be spatial and temporal. Kant's own answer is this: we can, indeed must, arrive at the firm belief that the world in itself is not deterministic, and so not spatial and temporal, on the basis of what practical reason requires.

Now it is time to draw together our journey so far. In the previous chapter I described to you the "solution" that Kant would arrive at. The promised solution was this: at a fundamental level of our existence, so fundamental that we can never directly experience it, we are non-spatial and non-temporal. This is where our freedom and our moral struggle *really* happens: in a non-spatial and non-temporal realm, of which our temporal biographies are in some sense derivative appearances. I ventured that this would not seem an immediately gripping account of our moral lives, but promised that by the end of this chapter, this "solution" would fall off the page as an elegant and satisfying way forward. Hopefully, in any case, we are able to understand how Kant could find some relief here, as he out-Platonizes the rationalists, and pushes true reality into a deep safety, while pulling the world of appearances out into the full enlightened glare of our own cognition. In this way, Kant protects, in one movement, both freedom and knowledge.

On his fourth day in purgatory, Dante steps onto the plateau of the mountain, the "earthly paradise":

> Eager now to explore in and about
> the luxuriant holy forest evergreen
> that softened the new light, I started out
>
> without delaying longer, from the stair
> and took my lingering way into the plain
> on ground that breathed a fragrance to the air.
> (Dante, *Purgatorio,* Canto XXVIII, lines 1-6)

Kant seems likewise ready now to lead us into his earthly paradise, with knowledge and freedom secure. But before accepting his invitation to climb the stair, a few things might trouble us about his proposed "solution." The next chapter addresses some of these concerns.

CHAPTER SIX

Interpreting Kant: Three Objections

In the concluding two chapters of this book we will step into Kant's earthly paradise, and properly look around, and appreciate why this "earthly paradise" is not paradise as such, and never could be. We will ask why Kant, like Virgil, withdraws before climbing into the realms of grace, revelation, and beatific vision. Dante's Virgil is unable to enter paradise. Virgil lives, with other pagan philosophers and poets, in the best neighborhood in hell, a "great citadel" with a "sweet brook" and a "green meadow," free of the infernal torments of the other circles in hell and illuminated by the soft but dignified half-lights of unaided human reason.

Before investigating Kant's earthly paradise, though, I want to address three objections or anxieties about Kant's solution as set out in the previous chapter. The responses offered to these anxieties should enrich our understanding of Kant's position. The first objection is more exegetical, disputing the interpretation presented here of Kant's critical philosophy. The second anxiety is that Kant's solution, if accepted, puts freedom and morality beyond the realm of the embodied, rendering them invisible, and perhaps even rather "spooky." The third worry is that if this is Kant's account, he is unable to explain our propensity to do other than the good.

Interpreting Kant's Transcendental Idealism

I have, in this part of the volume, been attempting to narrate the emergence of Kant's mature "critical" philosophy. The philosophical position explored in the previous chapter is known by the formidable title of "transcendental idealism." I have chosen to introduce the parameters of the position before using the terminology, and to do so in a narrative fashion, explaining the pressures on Kant's thought that lead him to the position. The alternative, I find, is for Kant's position to come across as a mixture of complex jargon and science fiction, with "transcendental idealism" instructing us that the mind "constructs reality" (all of it? even itself? even kidneys and amoeba?) but that reality in itself is non-spatial and non-temporal (why?), and that freedom and God (and what else?) are in this realm of reality-in-itself.

Having narrated the emergence of Kant's mature critical position, though, I have a responsibility to relate the account given here to the fierce and cyclical controversy in Kant studies about what precisely Kant's mature critical position is, or what "transcendental idealism" amounts to. It is important, because so much of the whole narrative set out here depends upon it, and because any reader approaching literature about or inspired by Kant will soon be exposed, explicitly or not, to one interpretation or another, in a way that will determine and shape the whole presentation. This section, which will have its challenges, will equip the reader to negotiate some of the interpretative issues at stake here.

First of all, we should discuss the intimidating term "transcendental idealism." This is best approached by taking each element of the description, and considering what each term is supposed to contrast with. First of all, the contrasting term to "transcendental" would be "empirical." Something is empirical if it pertains to that which appears and that which we experience. We might ask, though, what it is that makes the empirical possible? What underlies that which appears? Whatever this is, we can call "transcendental," meaning not that it is spooky and transcendent, but rather that it pertains to that which makes experience and knowledge possible. The contrasting term to "idealism" here would be "realism," whereby "realism" means, in this context, that something is independent of mind. "Idealism" means simply that which is dependent upon mind. So "transcendental idealism" points to the notion that experience and knowledge are possible only through the receptive and organizing activity of mind.

Only in two places in the first *Critique* does Kant explicitly define transcendental idealism.[1] The first definition goes as follows:

> I understand by the *transcendental idealism* of all appearances the doctrine that they are all together to be regarded as mere representations

---

1. I am indebted here to Henry Allison, "Kant's Transcendental Idealism," in *A Companion to Kant,* ed. Graham Bird (Oxford: Wiley-Blackwell, 2010), pp. 111-24 (p. 111).

and not things in themselves, and accordingly that time and space are only sensible forms of our intuition, but not determinations given for themselves or conditions of objects as things in themselves. To this idealism is opposed *transcendental realism,* which regards space and time as something given in themselves (independent of our sensibility). (A 369)

The second definition reads:

All objects of an experience possible for us, are nothing but appearances, i.e., mere representations, which, as they are represented, as extended beings or series of alterations, have outside our thoughts no existence grounded in itself. This doctrine I call transcendental idealism. (B 518-19)

Kant is keen to make several contrasts. Transcendental idealism is opposed, on the one hand, to "transcendental realism" which would make "mere representations into things in themselves" (B 518-19). Transcendental realism would claim that what makes possible experience ("transcendental") is thoroughly independent of the receptive activity of minds ("realism"). Kant is also keen to distinguish "transcendental" idealism from the "dogmatic" or "material" idealism of Berkeley ("reality just is a systematically ordered series of ideas"), and the "skeptical" or "empirical" idealism of Descartes ("all that we know of the world are ideas in our minds") (*Pr,* 4: 293, 373-75). Kant explains that transcendental idealism is merely "formal," in the sense that "it is a theory about the . . . 'forms' or conditions under which objects can be cognized by the human mind,"[2] rather than a knowledge claim about the fundamental conditions of reality itself.

This takes us so far, but ever since Kant's works have been read, from Kant's own time onward, there has been a recurring pattern to controversies about what exactly Kant means when he talks about "noumenal object/reality." Other synonyms that pick out this concept are "transcendental object," "intelligible object/reality," and "thing in itself." Speaking briskly, the interpretative options available are these: when Kant talks about noumenal reality and things in themselves (and other synonyms), (i) he does not really mean it; (ii) he does really mean it, and in so doing, goes beyond what he should talk about, according to his own system;

2. Allison, "Kant's Transcendental Idealism," p. 111.

(iii) he does really mean it, and in doing so, does not go beyond what he should talk about, according to his own system.

If you studied Kant in an Anglophone context in the 1970s or 1980s, it is likely you would be exposed to a version of (ii), as this was at the time an influential interpretation of Kant, supported by scholars such as Peter Strawson[3] and Jonathan Bennett.[4] If you were taught Kant in the 1990s or 2000s, it is more likely that you would be familiar with a version of (i), with a subtle and rigorous variation of this thesis put forward by Henry Allison.[5] Accounts that read Kant along the lines of (i) are sometimes called "deflationary" accounts, in that they "deflate" the seeming extravagance of Kant's references to an underlying unknowable reality. Just recently, (iii) has begun gathering some momentum. The reading of Kant offered here is strongly associated with (iii). Each of these interpretative options has a genealogy of exponents and supporters going back to Kant's own time, and so no resort to authority will carry the day.[6] Kant, I am convinced, was himself an exponent of (iii) about his own work, which perhaps carries some weight. Thinkers are not always right about what their thought implies or presupposes, but in this case, I am convinced, Kant was right. Although highly contested, the case for (iii) is, in my view (and I am not alone), overwhelming.[7]

3. Peter Strawson, *The Bounds of Sense: An Essay on Kant's Critique of Pure Reason* (London: Methuen, 1966).

4. Jonathan Bennett, *Kant's Analytic* (Cambridge: Cambridge University Press, 1966); and *Kant's Dialectic* (Cambridge: Cambridge University Press, 1974).

5. Henry Allison, *Kant's Transcendental Idealism: An Interpretation and Defense* (New Haven, CT: Yale University Press, 1983).

6. The reading of Kant that I support, which presents Kant as combining epistemic modesty and metaphysical commitments, can be found in a well-established German tradition, running through Heinz Heimsoeth and Max Wundt in the twentieth century, Erich Adickes and Karl Vaihinger in the nineteenth century, right back into the 1780s and 1790s, with Jena-based interpreters such as C. C. Schmid, Johann Erhard, Franz von Herbert, and Friedrich Niethammer. For a discussion of this group of Jena interpreters, to which I am indebted, see Karl Ameriks, *Kant and the Fate of Autonomy* (Cambridge: Cambridge University Press, 2000), pp. 64ff.

7. See, for example, Robert Adams, "Things in Themselves," *Philosophy and Phenomenological Research* 57.4 (1997): 801-25; Karl Ameriks, *Interpreting Kant's Critiques* (Oxford: Oxford University Press, 2003), chaps. 4 and 6; and his *Kant's Theory of Mind: An Analysis of the Paralogisms of Pure Reason* (Oxford: Oxford University Press, 2000); and Desmond Hogan, "Three Kinds of Rationalism and the Non-Spatiality of Things in Themselves," *Journal of the History of Philosophy* 47.3 (2009): 355-82; and his "How to Know Unknowable Things in Themselves," *Noûs* 43.1 (2009): 49-63.

Without entering an intricate scholarly debate, I want to say something about the rival interpretations, and why (iii) is to be preferred. As in chapter three, when I discussed the status of belief in God, my sense in relation to interpretation (i) is not that this interpretation is entirely wrong, but rather that it is not the whole truth, and the truth that it witnesses to can be better accommodated on the interpretation supported here. The most subtle and recent version of (i) is put forward by Henry Allison. Allison claims that when Kant talks about "things in themselves," this concept is intended merely as an heuristic category, a "shading" concept of the world as it is independently of our access to it, about which we cannot know or speculate. Why can we not know or meaningfully speculate about it? Well, because the instant we begin to speak about this world, we bring it within the pale of our conceptual schemas and categories, such that it is in principle no longer the world independent of our access to it. The "noumenal" realm of "things in themselves" is a constantly disappearing horizon, beyond the sphere of our attempts to grasp the world. Our inability to know or speak of this realm arises from its function in our thought as a constantly disappearing horizon, that which is always on the other side of our conceptual vista, rather than from any robust ontological theory of things in themselves underlying or being behind appearances.

In contrast to Allison's approach, the account I am presenting in this chapter would be called a "noumenal affection" interpretation of Kant. The "noumenal realm" is the ground of the world of appearances, whereby "noumenal objects" affect us. When they "appear to us," we call these appearances "phenomena" or "that which appears." These noumenal objects bring about our experience, which experience is always mediated through our forms of intuition, space, and time. Although we understand that our experience is always on this side of this mediation, coming downstream of how we receive the world, we also understand that it is dependent upon the world as it is in itself, even though we cannot know anything substantial about this world, except that it does indeed ground our experience. So as well as being committed to a notion of "noumenal affection," we also understand that we suffer from principled ignorance about noumenal reality. From the perspective of theoretical reason, we must acknowledge a "noumenal ignorance" about things in themselves.

Kant himself was presented with interpretations of his work that insisted that he could not really mean to say that there are noumenal objects that affect us. About such interpretations, Kant writes in 1790 that "the constant contention of the first *Critique*" is that

It posits this ground of the matter of sensory representations not once again in things, as objects of the senses, but in something super-sensible, which *grounds* the latter and of which we can have no cognition. It says that the objects as things-in-themselves *give* the matter to empirical intuitions (they contain the ground by which to determine the faculty of representation in accordance with its sensibility), but they *are* not the matter thereof. (*OD*, 8: 215)

In 1799, Kant refuses help from Fichte, after a reviewer claimed that "Fichte has realized what the *Critique* projected," by denying any noumenal affection:

Since the reviewer finally maintains that the *Critique* is not to be taken *literally* in what it says about sensibility and that anyone who wants to understand the *Critique* must first master the requisite *standpoint* (of Beck or Fichte), because *Kant's* precise words, like Aristotle's, will destroy the spirit, I therefore declare again that the *Critique* is to be understood by considering exactly what it says. (*DFW*, 12: 371)

In the early nineteenth century the commentator Vaihinger threw down a challenge to "any so-called Kantian with the nerve to assert, in the face of a hundred passages, that Kant never really said that there are unknown things in themselves which affect us."[8] The sorts of passages that Vaihinger had in mind are these:

How things in themselves may be (without regard to representations through which they affect us) is entirely beyond our cognitive sphere. (A 190/B 235)

Bodies are not objects in themselves that are present to us, but rather a mere appearance of who knows what unknown object. (A 387)

Meanwhile we can call the merely intelligible cause of appearances in general the transcendental object, merely so that we may have something corresponding to sensibility as a receptivity. To this transcendental object we can ascribe the whole extent and connection of our possible

8. Hans Vaihinger, *Commentar zu Kant's Kritik der reinen Vernunft*, vol. 2 (Stuttgart: W. Spemann und Union Deutsche Verlagsgesellschaft, 1881-92), pp. 5, 21.

perceptions and say that it is given in itself prior to all experience. But appearances are, in accordance with it, given not in themselves but only in this experience, because they are mere representations. (A 494/B 522)

For the existence of appearances ... demands that we look around us for something different from all appearances, hence for an intelligible object. (A 566/B 594)

If, on the other hand, appearances do not count for any more than that they are in fact, namely, not for things in themselves but only for mere representations connected in accordance with empirical laws, then they themselves must have grounds that are not appearances ... the intelligible cause, with its causality, is outside the series; its effects, on the contrary, are encountered in the series of empirical conditions. (A 537/B 565)

All that we can say about such noumenal objects is that they must ground our experience. We can say this with confidence, because our experience is a product of our reception of things as they are in themselves, and this reception cannot itself be the thing in itself that is received. The thing experienced is not the experience:

The transcendental object that grounds both outer appearances and inner intuition is neither matter nor a thinking being in itself, but rather an unknown ground of those appearances that supply us with our empirical concepts of the former as well as the latter. (A 380)

In ascribing to a "noumenal affection and ignorance" account of Kant, I align myself with other commentators such as Karl Ameriks. Ameriks gives a particularly perspicuous presentation of Kant's position that corresponds precisely with my presentation here, tracking Kant from his early to his late thought:

Kant starts [in early works] by going along with the common thought that there are things distinct from us. Then he subtracts from the intrinsic characterization of those things whatever features turn out not to be able to be consistently ascribed to them in that way. Finally, he concludes *not* that there is nothing, but rather that ... "something or other out there" still exists, and it is such that it cannot in itself have the specific spatiotemporal "forms" that our experience manifests. There is nothing absurd in saying all this while continuing to believe that distinct thing(s) in themselves definitely exist in contact with us, but that theoretically "we know not what" they are like otherwise in a positive way. . . . The main point here is that there is nothing in any of Kant's arguments about the ideality of spatiotemporality that ever involves *taking back* the most fundamental aspect of his starting position, which is simply the metaphysical claim that we are receptive to other things and there is something more than our individual finite being.[9]

When it comes to the needs of practical reason, this conceptual space of reality beyond appearances can be employed in order to ground our belief in freedom and morality. If space and time come downstream of our reception of the world, this means that we do not fundamentally come downstream of space and time, and the associated mechanism. So in the second *Critique* Kant writes:

The very same subject, being on the other side conscious of himself as a thing in itself, also views his existence *insofar as it does not stand under conditions of time* and himself as determinable only through laws that he gives himself by reason; and in this existence of his nothing is, for him, antecedent to the determination of his will, but every action — and in general every determination of his existence changing conformably with inner sense, even the whole sequence of his existence as a sensible being — is to be regarded in the consciousness of his intelligible existence as nothing but the consequence and never as the determining ground of his causality as a *noumenon*. So considered, a rational being can now rightly say of every unlawful action he performed that he could have omitted it even though as appearance it is sufficiently determined in the past and, so far, is inevitably necessary; for this action, with all the past which determines it, belongs to a single phenomenon of his character, which he gives to himself and in accordance with which he imputes to himself, as a cause independent of all sensibility, the causality of those appearances. (*CPrR*, 5: 97-98)

In the 1790s Kant writes further about an (unknowable) noumenal causation that is our freedom. In *Religion within the Boundaries of Mere*

9. Ameriks, *Interpreting Kant's Critiques*, p. 29.

Reason, Kant explains that "the propensity to evil" is an "intelligible deed, cognizable through reason alone apart from any temporal condition" (*Rel,* 6: 31), where the "sensible, empirical" (*Rel,* 6: 31) appearance of this "intelligible deed" appears as a "deed contrary to law" (*Rel,* 6: 31). In his 1794 text, *The End of All Things,* Kant reflects on this notion of a timeless noumenal disposition *(Gesinnung):*

> Nothing remains for us but to think of an endlessly progressing change in the constant progress toward our final end, through which our *attitude* remains always the same. (But our attitude is not, like this progress, a phenomenon; rather it is something supersensible, and so does not alter in time). (*EaT,* 8: 334)[10]

Some commentators worry that Kant is being inconsistent in talking about a type of causation beyond space and time, when all the causation we *know* about occurs in space and time. Kant has an answer to this, which relies on his drawing out the different textures of assent that we can give to propositions. Not all types of assent, and perhaps not the most important ones, are knowledge. We cannot *know* about noumenal causation, but we can certainly hold beliefs about it. Kant is crystal clear on this:

> The categories are not restricted in *thinking* by the conditions of our sensible intuition, but have an unbounded field, and only the *cognition* of objects that we think, the determination of the object, requires intuition; in the absence of the latter, the thought of the object can still have its true and useful consequences for the use of the subject's reason, which, however, cannot be expounded here, for it is not always directed to the determination of the object, thus to cognition, but rather also to that of the subject and its willing. (B 166n)

This permission to think beyond the bounds of knowledge is reiterated in 1797, when Kant insists that "the category of causation" can be applied by practical reason "in the relation of supersensible beings," that is to say, to us as noumenal realities. We apply the category of causation, but without reference to a *"temporal condition"* (*MetM,* 6: 280n). We use

10. Here I use the translation given by Allen W. Wood in "Kant's Compatibilism," in *Self and Nature in Kant's Philosophy,* ed. Allen W. Wood (Ithaca, NY: Cornell University Press, 1984), p. 98, rather than the translation, also by Wood, in the Cambridge Edition.

the "pure category" of causation "without a schema put under it," by which Kant means the pure category of causation/grounding, abstracted from our spatial and temporal ways of receiving the world.

What we find is that "transcendental idealism," on the "noumenal affection and ignorance" interpretation, has three dimensions. It sets the limits to knowledge. Within those limits, knowledge is made secure. It opens up possibilities for thinking beyond those limits, once it is understood that what is within the limits need not apply to that which goes beyond the limits. That is to say, transcendental idealism retains epistemic humility about what we can know, while opening up the possibility that the way things are is fundamentally different from the way things appear to be. Things appear to be determined, but this is just an appearance. We can hold out the belief in freedom without epistemic irresponsibility.

I said above that the deflationary approach, with reference to noumenal objects, was "not entirely wrong." What I mean here is this: exponents of the deflationary approach emphasize that references to noumenal/intelligible/transcendental objects have a shading effect on what we can experience and know, gesturing to the world beyond and behind what can be experienced and known. This is correct, I think. On the noumenal affection and ignorance approach recommended here, we expect the language of noumenal objects to have such a shading effect. We look at a tree, the thing known and seen, and we know that there must be some sort of noumenal grounding, but more than this we do not know. The "noumenal reality" that underlies the tree does indeed do no more than shade our concept of the tree that appears, the "phenomenal tree." Any further investigation that we undertake on the tree will be on the side of "that which appears," exploring more finely grained and intricate textures of this appearing.

Passages that are often cited in favor of the more deflationary reading are in fact easily accommodated by the noumenal affection reading. In fact, they can be incorporated into that reading and made part of the interpretative case. For example, in the "Transcendental Aesthetic" of the first *Critique,* Kant writes that space "signifies nothing" except as "that through which we may be affected by objects" (A 26/B 42):

This predicate can be ascribed to things only insofar as they appear to us [and] space comprehends all things that may appear to us externally, but not all things in themselves. (A 27/B 43)

This passage, and others like it (A 11-12/B 25; A 32-33/B 49; A 48/B 65; A 369; A 491/B 518-19), explain that because space and time are features of our reception, and not of things in themselves, we can open up the conceptual possibility of freedom at a fundamental level. This is one aspect of transcendental idealism on the noumenal affection account, as interpreted above. In the section entitled "Phenomena and Noumena," Kant explains:

> The principles of pure understanding can apply only to objects of the senses under the universal conditions of a possible experience, never to things in general without regard to the mode in which we are able to intuit them. (A 246/B 303)

Once again, this tells us that principles of understanding, such as spatio-temporal causation, are relevant to "the mode in which we are able to intuit them" (A 246/B 303). Again, this opens up the freedom to think about a level of fundamental reality that is not locked into deterministic patterns of causation.

When the debate between the deflationary and the noumenal affection interpretations is sometimes set up, there can be an implication that there are two sorts of passages in Kant's texts, in relation to noumenal objects: passages that imply noumenal affection, and passages that require a deflationary "shading" account. The suggestion is that any interpreter has to choose which set of passages to prioritize, and which set of passages to edit out, or at least, give a subordinate role to. Given that the "deflationary" approach is more amenable to a naturalistic mindset, the choice in favor of the deflationary passages then seems clear. In a way that is structurally similar to the debate about the highest good and belief in God (discussed in chapter three), this is not an accurate presentation of the interpretative situation. The passages cited in favor of the deflationary approach can be easily accommodated by the noumenal affection and ignorance account, and incorporated as part of the case for this interpretation. On the other hand, passages that require a noumenal affection interpretation cannot be so easily accommodated by deflationary approaches. The option, therefore, is not between one set of Kant passages or the other, but between accommodating all the passages, or only some of them. I submit that we should prefer an interpretation that can accommodate as many passages as possible from texts intended by the author as a unity, and that this accommodation should be achieved, where possible, without deflating or downgrading these passages in ways that are not explicitly demanded by

Kant himself. Application of this principle favors the noumenal affection interpretation.

That noumenal affection accounts can accommodate supposedly "deflationary" passages is important, as it undercuts a standard criticism of noumenal affection accounts. This criticism assumes that noumenal affection accounts are committed to what is sometimes called a "two world interpretation" of Kant, where one world is non-spatial and non-temporal (the "noumenal realm"), and the other world (the "phenomenal realm") is spatial and temporal. Noumenal affection accounts, it is claimed, are committed to the view that "somehow" non-spatial and non-temporal things in themselves interact with the world of spatial and temporal things. All manner of problems cluster around the nature and coherence of the causal relationship supposedly envisaged by Kant, on this "two world interpretation," between spatio-temporal and non-spatio-temporal realities.

Such a picture is not at all what Kant has in mind, and it is not what a plausible noumenal affection account should claim. Part of the problem here is a now standard taxonomy for classifying interpretations of transcendental idealism ("one world or two"), which can be found in learned journals, monographs, and textbooks. This taxonomy is in fact deeply unhelpful, not least because it solidifies the assumption that "one world" interpretations must be "epistemological rather than metaphysical," with no trace of traditional metaphysics, and that more metaphysically committed interpretations are freighted with all the difficulties of the "two world" interpretation, as set out above. Kant's position meets these two rival models rather like a three-dimensional object passing through two-dimensional planes. Rather than starting with the problematic distinction, and fitting Kant into this, it is better just to state Kant's position, gesturing to aspects of this position that both camps have partially understood.

Theologically sensitive noumenal affection accounts understand that we are dealing with one created world (so far, so good, for "one world" accounts), which therefore does not include the uncreated God, who is not part of any world. This is not typically addressed at all by one world accounts, which tend to occlude any sort of traditional metaphysics. God, who is not part of the "world" (or any other world), creates the world, which is the realm of things in themselves. Among these things in themselves are ourselves. Our reception of things in themselves, both of our own noumenal selves and of other things, is always and everywhere mediated through the forms of intuition, space, and time, and the categories of thought (such as substance and causation), insofar as these are received through space and time. There are degrees of appearance and disclosure to rational creatures who are part of the created (noumenal) world, where "epistemic humility" consists in understanding the principled boundaries of what we can and cannot know within this framework, and what we must rationally believe, given these boundaries, alongside our non-negotiable commitment to irreducibly important projects such as morality.

The relevant distinction (as one world interpretations typically emphasize) is indeed between things as they are in themselves, and things as they appear: and the distinction applies from top-to-bottom and everywhere. The whole event of our being affected by a spatio-temporal object is the appearance of a more fundamental noumenal interaction (although we know not what). There is no mysterious interaction between spatio-temporal and non-spatio-temporal objects, although there is a spatio-temporal appearing of fundamentally non-spatio-temporal objects. Standard one world interpretations tend to occlude (whereas two world interpretations emphasize) Kant's undoubted fundamental commitment to things in themselves being non-spatial and non-temporal. This does not lead to extravagant metaphysical speculation, as we could never in principle know how spatial and temporal objects "map" onto things in themselves. Does an empirical tree in some sense "correspond," in a one-to-one way, with a thing in itself? We know that our experience of a tree is somehow answerable to and determined by a supersensible reality, but the mechanism of the grounding is inaccessible to us. We simply cannot know what it is (singular or plural) that grounds the appearance that is a tree. That, we might say, is the whole point, as the claim that there *must* be a one-to-one correspondence between the objects of experience and things in themselves risks violating the very epistemic discipline that one world interpretations value so highly. We can, though, on the basis of the rational and disciplined needs of practical reason come to warranted beliefs about the realm of things in themselves, as long as these beliefs do not contradict what theoretical reason is able to know.

Spookiness

Perhaps enough has been said in defense of the interpretation of Kant's position that I narrate in this book. But then we are led to a second anxiety. The second anxiety is this: even if we accept the broad parameters of the interpretation offered here, and even if we can now see how Kant is "forced" to his solution, his account of freedom and our moral struggle has an eerie, spooky, ghostly, and unreal quality. Consider: our freedom, and our real moral struggle, occurs always and everywhere behind and beyond the realm of appearances. Our freedom is, in principle, "invisible," in that it never appears in the spatial-temporal world of our experience or thoughts. All our actions, including our thoughts and interpretations, are appearances of something (we know not what) that is happening at a more fundamental level. Would not such a worldview, if embraced, make us radically and culpably uninterested in whole swathes of reality: emotions, thoughts, bodies, culture, history, society, psychology, anthropology?

To help us think about this objection, imagine the following scenario. Your boiler needs fixing, so you call a plumber. The plumber arrives, and as he removes the front from the boiler, he explains delightedly that he is a Kantian, which he goes on to explain involves the conviction that space and time, and all the causal mechanisms involved in making the boiler work, are features of our reception of the world, rather than being in the world in itself. "Isn't it amazing?" he declares, holding up his hands, pointing at the inner mechanism of the boiler.

Now, would you trust this man to fix your boiler? Well, why not? What matters is that the plumber, as well as being a Kantian, is devotedly concerned about, and expert in, the way in which the noumenal substrate to boilers and their parts (whatever that is) make its/their appearance. There would be a cause for concern if the plumber was only a Kantian some of the time, or about bits of the boiler — maybe parts that he found a bit unfathomable — or if the plumber thought that an implication of his Kantianism was that his mind could somehow change the structure of the laws of mechanism germane to plumbing, or that by concentrating he could make the wrong part become the right part.

A striking feature of Kant's thought, when one considers the whole corpus of his writings and lectures, is indeed his insatiable fascination with every aspect of the way in which phenomenal reality unfolds. It is well known that Kant's position on space and time does not prevent him from being fascinated with the structure and mechanisms of Newtonian science. Less well known, but no less true, is that he is equally fascinated by empirical psychology, anthropology, politics, history, theories of education, and culture. As we have seen with rationalism and Platonism more generally, believing that the fundamental structure of reality is quite different from the way reality appears need in no way reduce one's appetite for understanding and studying every texture of the appearance. And certainly, there is never any suggestion that our minds or wills have "control" over the realm of appearances, any more than they do over the world as it is in itself. Appearances are grounded not on our wills, but on things as they fundamentally are, even if this is mediated through space and time.

Nor does such an interest in the texture of appearances indicate that one's rationalism, with its Platonic resonances, is in crisis. That underlying reality is quite different from appearances is precisely what one would expect: in a way, that's the whole point. We have perhaps a partial contemporary corollary, in the way in which we accept what physicists tell us, that the fundamental structure of reality — quarks, electrons, void, dark matter — is quite different from what appears. This does not make us, or the physicist, less interested in or committed to our ordinary embodied and culturally embedded existence.

Nor would it be quite right to say that underlying reality, for the rationalist, or for the Platonist, is "remote" from our experience. The underlying reality does not make an appearance at any particular point, but it is not somewhere "else." Rather, noumenal reality underlies that which appears everywhere. So it is for Kant: freedom is never somewhere in space and time, because it always and everywhere underlies the whole realm of appearances. Rather like God on classical conceptions, our freedom is equally intimate and present to each moment of our spatial and temporal biography.

What we come back to is that Kant's fundamental worldview is not best understood as a dualism between the deep "spooky" fundamental level of reality and "another realm" of spatial and temporal objects. There is just one created realm, with different degrees of unveiling of the depths and intensities of creation. Holding this model in our minds enables us to locate and place in perspective a standard debate in Kant studies as to whether or not the mature Kant is in fact still a "compatibilist" (as discussed in chapter four). The reason some commentators think that Kant is a compatibilist is this: compatibilism claims that our being determined is not incompatible with our being considered free.[11] Kant's mature posi-

---

11. For recent discussions on different sides of the terminological issue, see Simon Shengjian Xie, "What Is Kant: A Compatibilist or an Incompatibilist? A New Interpretation of Kant's Solution to the Free Will Problem," *Kant-Studien* 100.1 (2009): 53-76; and Coleen P. Zoller, "The Pre-Critical Roots of Kant's Compatibilism," *Philosophy and Theology* 19.1-2 (2007): 197-213. Xie focuses on the ultimate responsibility required by Kant's transcendental freedom, and the fact that we can do otherwise, but neglects that the ability to do otherwise is not essential for freedom as such. Zoller concentrates on Kant's intellectualist

tion claims that on the level of phenomenal appearances, we are indeed "determined," in that the whole realm of phenomena can be understood in deterministic terms, but that nonetheless we are still free at a more fundamental and noumenal level. With a nice subtlety, Allen Wood explains that Kant's position is best described as a "compatibilism" between "compatibilism" on the one hand, and "non-compatibilism" on the other:[12] the phenomenal realm is determined, although we can speak of "free actions" in a compatibilist way, but this is compatible with non-compatibilism operating at a noumenal level. As always with these things, it depends upon what you mean; but we should also attend to misleading associations that might crowd around one's intended meaning. There is a texture to Kant's thought ("that which appears") that looks to be deterministic, and a texture to his thought that sustains, at the noumenal level, a non-compatibilist account of freedom. In a sense, we could indeed say that Kant runs both determinism and freedom together, and so is "compatibilist." But it will nearly always be misleading to say this. This is because compatibilism usually indicates a view where determinism has the upper hand: where the fundamental furniture of the universe is construed as determined, but where this is, in some sense, not incompatible with our using the concept of freedom. Kant's worldview turns this on its head: at a deep and fundamental level there is non-compatibilist freedom. The determinism (the "compatibilism") that appears is derivative upon this more originary freedom, and is a feature not of the world in itself, but of our reception of the world in spatial and temporal terms. Our non-compatibilist freedom is invisible, but more fundamental and originary, with determinism being a derivative unveiling, and veiling, of a more fundamental reality.

Evil

But now we hit a really deep mystery. Our freedom is to be found beyond the constraints of space and time, which also means that it is beyond sensuous impulses and temptations. If we are to think of ourselves in this space of freedom, we can think of ourselves in a sort of community with other

---

notion of perfect freedom, which involves following the moral law, whether or not one can do otherwise. Zoller is correct to perceive this continuity in the concept of freedom, although she neglects the shift from the pre-critical to the critical Kant, whereby Kant begins to ascribe to us ultimate responsibility for whether or not we follow the moral law.

12. Wood, "Kant's Compatibilism," pp. 73-101.

free beings, all of whom are in community with God. This is, in fact, as I will show in the final two chapters, how Kant does conceive of our freedom. But then we ask: how does evil come into the picture? Or, in terms of one of the framing questions of this book, how does it come about that we can use our freedom in such a way that we violate our search for the highest good, where our highest good involves our ability to become what we ought to be? We are beyond the realm of temptation, and live only with other rational noumenal selves. The world of temptation, degradation, and suffering is, we know, somehow grounded upon ultimate reality, and so we do know that our noumenal selves, ourselves as we really are, do indeed turn away from the good, toward destructive self-love. But how or why "we" could or would ever do that remains inscrutable.

Here we see that human freedom has been aligned with divine freedom in one sense, in that we, like God, are "ultimately responsible" for our actions. We also remember from chapters two and three that God is unable to do other than the good. But we *can* do other than the good. I think that Kant considers this feature of our freedom to be undeniable. Just look around: we do, at a fundamental level, do other than the good, and the consequences unfold in the realm of appearances. But it remains, for Kant, regrettable that we have this ability. He writes in the 1780s that "although the human being . . . can always decide something else," it is "precisely this which is a lack of freedom in the human being, since he does *not always* act according to his reason," whereas it is "true freedom in God that he decides only what is in conformity with his highest understanding" (*LPR*, 28: 1068).

Conclusion

We finish then with a double mystery, and a real problem for Kant's "solution." Why was this freedom so worth the intellectual struggle, if what we have won is, as Kant puts it in another text, "a loss," leading Kant to reflect that the "history" of human freedom "begins with evil" (*CHH*, 8: 107-23)? Perhaps Kant comes to this position just because he considers it to be, regrettably, a consequence of our being genuinely free, where we are ultimately responsible for our actions. Perhaps it might have been better not to be able to do other than the good, but, manifestly, this is not the freedom that was given to us. The second facet of the mystery is less easy to answer. Why and how do we ever go wrong? Even if we permit Kant's "solution," it seems there is no conceptual space for understanding a motiveless turning away from the good, which must come from our sheer pointless willing of that which is not good.

Kant, honest to the last, does not flinch from his inability to give an account of why and how we use our freedom to turn away from the good, from what it is that we ought to be. In 1794 Kant writes that "evil can have originated only from moral evil (not just from the limitations of our nature)," but that our "original predisposition" as created by God "is a predisposition to the good." "None other than the human being," Kant writes, "could have corrupted" this nature, but "there is no conceivable ground for us" from which "moral evil could first have come in us" (*Rel,* 6: 43). Kant describes the account of the fall given in Genesis as the expression of "this incomprehensibility in a historical narrative," where the "absolutely *first* beginning of all evil" (in the serpent) is "represented as incomprehensible to us (for whence the evil in that spirit?)," and where the human being is "represented as having lapsed" only "*through temptation,* hence not as corrupted *fundamentally,*" so that "there still remains hope of a return to the good from which he has strayed" (*Rel,* 6: 44).

In the "ancient holy wood" in the earthly paradise at the top of purgatory, Dante meets Matilda, who represents the active life of the soul, which incorporates our free will. Matilda explains to Dante:

> That Highest Good which only Itself can please
> made man good, and for goodness, and It gave him
> this place as earnest of eternal peace.
>
> But man defaulted. All too brief his stay.
> Defaulted, and exchanged for tears and toil
> his innocent first laughter and sweet play.
>
> (Dante, *Purgatorio,* Canto XXVIII, lines 91-96)

Matilda talks here of "this place" as Eden, indicating that the earthly paradise is in fact one, symbolically, with the Garden of Eden. At the end of his struggle, as Kant steps into the sunlight, he is back in precarious Eden. We are created by God, free, and with a predisposition to the good, yet always about to fall. In the final two chapters, we will watch unfold the incomprehensible turn, first away from the good, and then back toward it. When explaining free will, Virgil tells Dante, "As far as reason sees / I can reply. The rest you must ask Beatrice. The answer lies within faith's mysteries."

It will become clear that Kant, like Virgil, sees as far as reason sees.

CHAPTER SEVEN

The Dancer and the Dance: Divine Action, Human Freedom

Let us say, with Kant, that freedom involves our being ultimately responsible for our actions, and being able to do other than we do. Let us also say, with Kant, that the highest good involves becoming what we ought to be, achieving our purpose, flourishing in our properly ordered rational human nature. This is the source of a tension at the heart of Kant's philosophy: freedom, our ability to do what we want, although essential for human autonomy, is also corrosive of our ability and calling to become what we ought to be. We might, perhaps, explore the concept of human freedom through the metaphor of dancing. A dance is something that we do volitionally. It can be rule-governed, where our movements are shaped by these rules. We can also be steered and led by someone else. All the time, the dance remains an expression of freedom.

> O body swayed to music, O brightening glance,
> How can we know the dancer from the dance?
> (W. B. Yeats, "Among School Children")

To answer W. B. Yeats's question, one sure way to distinguish the dancer from the dance is when the dancer is terrible: tripping, stumbling, cursing his partner, walking moodily off the dance floor. In this chapter, I set out a thesis about freedom, by engaging with Kant and the premodern theological tradition. The thesis, in a nutshell, is this. Kant is quite a bad dancer. But he is no worse than anyone else on the dance floor. When you are a bad dancer, the best course of action is to know this, and to hope that you will be led in the dance, and by the dance, rather than to attempt to see it out with bravado, boasting, and glitter-balls. Kant, to his credit, knows he is a bad dancer, and does not put on the bravado; but nor does he allow himself to hope that he will be led in the dance.

The "hope of being led in the dance" involves hoping that our freedom will be led, so that our every movement arises from the true dancer, and every movement is both ours and the other's, but only truly ours — expressive of what we most desire — because it is led by the other, who alone knows how to sway to the music, and how to become the dance. For the pre-modern tradition, the identity of the true dancer, and the name of the dance, are the same: God. In a few lines from "A Prayer for My Daughter," Yeats perhaps gestures toward this moment in the tradition:

> Considering that, all hatred driven hence,
> The soul recovers radical innocence
> And learns at last that it is self-delighting,
> Self-appeasing, self-affrighting,
> And that its own sweet will is Heaven's will
>
> (Yeats, "A Prayer for My Daughter")

The account of human freedom supported by the premodern tradition is a mystery of faith. Kant, like Dante's Virgil, is unable to go beyond purgatory. He "sees as reason sees," and cannot permit himself this hope based upon mystery. In this chapter, I will engage with Kant, by making a case for mystery, as a rationally satisfying, but not compelling or coercive, expression of studied and intelligible bafflement at our inability to do that which we most desire.

We saw in the last chapter that at the end of all his struggles, Kant seems to have spiraled his way up to our first beginning: a sort of eternal Eden, where human beings, now ultimately responsible for their actions, stand precariously on the precipice of their ability to do other than the good. As we have seen, our ability to do other than the good, that there are things other than the good, is, for Kant, a "regrettable" feature of our being ultimately responsible for our actions. We have also seen that Kant is convinced both that we do have this ability to do other than the good, and that this ability is the only way to secure that which really is important: our ultimate responsibility for our actions, and our being the spontaneous and original first cause. We are able to use our originary freedom, on the one hand, to choose the good, to become autonomous, where we become what we ought to be, which leads to happiness as a necessary consequence; or we can choose other than the good, which leads to various forms of enslavement and misery. This much is clear for the mature Kant: whichever it is, the choice must be *ours and ours alone*. We must not be acted upon by God, by other creatures, or by mechanistic chains of cause and effect. Such radical independence will make dancing difficult.

As a literary device, providing vivid images for complex philosophical trajectories and influences, I have drawn an analogy between Kant's intellectual journey and Dante's journey up the mountain of purgatory, accompanied by Virgil. As I explained in the introduction, there is some justice to the analogy, in that Virgil, for Dante, represents what unaccompanied human reason can achieve in relation to divine truths. One of the truths of Christianity that Virgil, or reason as such, is able to understand is that we must indeed be responsible for our actions, which involves being able to do other than we do. But there is a deeper mystery which Dante tells us Virgil cannot understand, where Dante in fact speaks for the whole premodern theological tradition: which is that our being ultimately responsible for our actions, and even — in a sense — our being able to do otherwise, is entirely compatible with divine action, our divine dancer, being at the beginning and end of all our actions.

This mystery is only approached once Virgil has departed, and Dante enters paradise with Beatrice as his guide. Consider again the claim I made above: "this much is clear, for the mature Kant: the choice must be *ours and ours alone*. We must not be acted upon by God, by other creatures, or by mechanistic chains of cause and effect." What the premodern theological tradition would say here is rather this: "the choice must be *ours and ours alone,* where we are not acted upon by other creatures, or by mechanistic chains of cause and effect, but where all the freedom we ever have is a consequence of God constantly and everywhere acting in our actions." God, and God alone, can act entirely in every one of our actions, without this reducing our freedom at all. This traditional account of divine action in relation to the action of creatures is called concurrence, or concursus; the Latin etymology goes back to the notion of "running together," where God's "concurring" action is an action that can always in some sense "run with" human action. We need to be careful here not to say "running alongside," or not only to say this. As we will see, we also need to include more mysterious connotations of "running together by being within."

Is this hard to understand? Well, in a sense, good: it is supposed to be. It is one of the mysteries of faith, beyond the grasp of reason. Kant knows about this conception of divine action in relation to human action, or at least he knows something about it, and he rejects it. You might have expected this. We have seen that Kant is well able to go "beyond" knowledge; but we have not heard at all from Kant, so far, about going beyond *reason*. The work in which Kant addresses Christian doctrines such as grace and atonement is called *Religion within the Boundaries of Reason Alone,* and religion beyond the boundaries of reason is not a place that Kant really wants to go. Kant's rejection of this mystery about divine action creates a huge rupture with the earlier tradition, and is of enormous significance, I would argue, for weighing up Kant's legacy for theology, and for our thinking about freedom and autonomy, as well as for our thinking about how we go about thinking at all.

At the beginning of this book, I proposed to treat Kant's religious thought with full integrity, which involved not dragging Kant to the baptism font. I proposed that Kant was a sort of Christianized Platonist, with the Platonism mediated through theological rationalism, but not perhaps a Christian Platonist. What prevents Kant from being called a Christian Platonist is his denial, neglect, or ignorance about core dimensions of the Christian tradition: for example, incarnation, trinity, divine simplicity, and the concursus between divine action and human action. In the second chapter, I suggested that in this space between Kant's religious ethic, and a Christian ethic, theologians are entitled to engage with Kant on immanently theological terms. In this chapter, I intensify this engagement.

I do not propose to take Kant through the list just set out: incarnation, trinity, divine simplicity, and concursus. Rather, I want to think a little about what might underlie Kant's reluctance to engage with all and any doctrine that goes, in his terms, "beyond reason." In fact, I am going to attempt what seems, on first blush, to be a perilous exercise, of presenting reasons in favor of "going beyond reason."

There is a distinction here, between a crazy thing that might be meant by "going beyond reason," and a more nuanced thing. I think we already have a good sense of the night terrors that the notion of "going beyond reason" might have for Kant: it evokes Swedenborgian reveries of talking to spirits, and paranormal powers of perception and prediction. I do not want to go beyond reason in this sense, and neither does any Christian theologian, traditional or contemporary, that I know of. Swedenborg is the *bête-noire* not only for Kant perhaps, but for all thinkers, metaphysical and theological, who go beyond the observable, or beyond the rational. My argument with Kant is that this is not the only sense in which one might "go beyond reason." When a Christian theologian such as Aquinas talks of the mysteries of faith which go beyond reason, this is not intended as an authoritarian and irrational appeal to that for which we have no evidence, or that which makes no sense, which reason should disapprove of. Aquinas is not chatting away to aristocratic shades about receipts for silverware. Rather, Aquinas is talking about an appeal to that which reason most deeply desires and knows that it lacks, longing to be led in the dance that it cannot perform alone. "Mystery" is not the same as nonsense, known contradictions, guess-work, or wishful thinking. What is it then? In the first part of this chapter I will try to answer this question, with reference to one particular issue, the relationship between divine action and human freedom.

This is how my argument will go. First of all, I present some analogies to free our minds a little. Second, I offer an exploration of how "mystery" works in Aquinas, in relation to rationality, with reference to the issue of human freedom. Third, I set out an account of the grounds for Kant's rejection of this account of human freedom. Finally, I suggest that on the issue of freedom, we can never escape mystery, and that there is a wis-dom in knowingly living within this unknowing. This does not show that Christianity is true, or even coherent; but it does show that there might be wisdom in a studied announcement that our freedom is for us a gift, a mystery, a puzzle, and a problem. Attempts to resolve the puzzle with human rational solutions are always precarious. Invoking God does not provide a "solution," but refuses false resolutions, by naming our struc-tural ignorance and inability, repeating again and again, "not us," "not us," "never us alone." Even the non-believer can accept the significance of the God concept here, as an announcement of the need for transcendence, even if they do not permit themselves the hope for it.

Going "Beyond Reason"

First of all, I present some analogies, which I acknowledge are only slightly more precise than the dancing metaphor, but which might help us to approach what the Christian tradition can mean by going "beyond reason." The art of human happiness is "beyond mathematics," which is not to say that it violates mathematics, or is something that mathematics will disapprove of. Indeed, the mathematician will understand that the art of human happiness is beyond its reach. The second analogy: in our deepest longing for another human being, we achieve our fulfillment by forgetting ourselves. In going beyond our egoism, we do not do violence to our self, rather we become what we ought to be. Analogously, we might ask whether reason can achieve its end by reaching beyond itself. Could reason be brought to the point of seeing and understanding a need to surpass itself, and to be gripped by the truth of something beyond its remit? Reason will not follow, but knows this as a limitation in itself, rather than a flaw in the path that lies beyond it. When Virgil talks of the truths that he, seeing as reason sees, is unable to expound to Dante, he bows his head, "sorrowing and silent": "be satisfied with the [because] of cause unknown / O humankind!'" (Dante, *Purgatorio,* Canto III, lines 45, 37-38). Virgil speaks poignantly here of Aristotle and Plato, "of them and many more," indicating himself among the number who have had to "yearn endlessly in vain" in their desire for truth, "but have, instead, its hunger as their pain" (*Purgatorio,* Canto III, lines 40-45). It is not Dante who leaves Virgil, but Virgil who leaves Dante, pushing him to the gate he is not permitted to pass. Having led Dante to the boundary of what reason can achieve, he presses him to go on, to meet Beatrice, "who will become," Virgil promises, "your lamp / between the truth and mere intelligence" (*Purgatorio,* Canto III, lines 47-48). Faith's mysteries are the lamp between the truth and mere intelligence, and as truth is intelligible and the source of intelligence, these mysteries have a shape that reason can recognize and trace, while knowingly being unable to grasp.

If Kant is our Virgil, Aquinas is our Beatrice, setting out the mystery of divine action and human freedom. To hear what Aquinas has to say, I think it helps to reflect a little on the way in which much of our ordinary everyday thinking works. When Aquinas holds up the lamp of faith's mysteries, the light thrown out casts a defining shadow, helping us dimly to discern something about all our creaturely efforts at understanding our place in the world. In our ordinary thinking, many of us will gravitate toward various magnetic poles. Many of us will think that, in some sense, equality is an important value. We will also, many of us, value freedom, in some sense. It is well known that freedom and equality can lead in different directions: my freedom to accumulate vast wealth will inevitably lessen equality. Similarly, many of us will value civil liberties, the right to free speech, free association, and non-interference from the state; but we will also value security. Again, it is well known that civil liberties and security can lead in different directions.

Some philosophers, or practitioners, will try to arrive a higher-level resolution, and some of these will do so by eliminating one of the poles altogether. So, for example, everything can become subordinated to state security, or we allow unbridled liberty, no matter what the impact on equality.

If this does violence to our pre-philosophical intuitions, so much the worse for these intuitions, says a certain type of philosopher. When presented with such philosophical zeal toward coherence, where pre-philosophical intuitions are offered up to the bonfire of consistency, I would submit that we have grounds to be worried. Crushing our pre-philosophical intuitions in order to save a particular theory or explanation can be a route to philosophically sophisticated rigidity of thought, or even ideology.

In any case, whether or not it is always desirable, I put it to you, most of our thinking and practice, most of the time, goes on in some sort of unresolved space between these magnetic poles: freedom and equality, liberty and security, or fill in your own favorite dilemma. Much of the time we do not know how to hold the poles together properly, and we do not have a higher-level theory which precisely quantifies and balances freedom and equality, or civil liberties and security. As Wittgenstein says, a precise picture of a blurred reality is a distortion, not an improvement. So, it might be better not to have a fully resolved theory, and to know that we do not. What we have is a shape, within which we must do our thinking and our acting. Each side of the shape has an intelligible rationale, which can be set out and understood. What cannot be fully understood always is how all the intelligible edifices that make up the shape precisely relate to one another.

This, I put it to you, is a natural and unavoidable feature of the ordinary way in which we form and hold beliefs. Theological thinking is no exception and, in fact, throws light on ordinary thinking, because it can be so aware and self-reflexive about how our humble creaturely beliefs are so clumsily formed, in stark contrast to the divine mind who knows in the same movement as creating. For Aquinas, we are the dumbest of the rational creatures in the universe, coming after God and the angels. We are so dumb that we require example after example in order to learn anything at all: hence we need to experience bodies, the particular examples of eternal essences, in order to get to know anything about them, while God and the angels can simply know the essences.

Concurrence

We can build up to the mystery of faith that is a concurrence account of divine action and human freedom, by building up two edifices, each of them intelligible and rational in its own terms, within which theological thinking must occur. It is when we try, and fail, to relate each of these edifices, that we know that we must go beyond reason, and that we are being shown a lamp between the truth and mere intelligence. This is how "mystery" might work, and it is not the same as a Swedenborgian apparition or a sheer resort to authority.

The first edifice is this. God, according to Christian theology, is the creator *ex nihilo,* who creates everything that is from nothing. This is in distinction from some non-Christianized Neoplatonic conceptions, for example, which think of everything that is as a necessary, and so non-free and non-distinct, emanation of an uncreated God. This conception is also distinct from other non-Christianized Neoplatonic accounts, where everything is formed by a demiurge, who shapes preexistent matter, without creating it from nothing. Perhaps we too quickly think we know what creation *ex nihilo* really involves. Where we can fail to push deeply enough is in thinking about the meaning of the word "everything" in the claim that God "creates everything." There can be a tendency to envisage the "everything" here as "medium-sized objects" or "substances" or "things." God creates things, which then sort of have a life of their own.

Classical Christianity is much stranger than this. Think of it like this. Take the room or space you are sitting in right now, and freeze it in a sort of ontological snapshot, that is to say, a snapshot of everything in the room that has "being" *(ontos).* What, might we say, is in the picture? What are the different "ontological textures," or the ways in which things have being? Certainly, there might be things: tables, chairs, lights, people. Also there will be forms of movement and change, from microscopic chemical reactions, to visible things, perhaps a clock hand, or the breeze on the curtains. Also there are actions, some involuntary, and others voluntary. There are also thoughts, some silent, others expressed. Behind these thoughts, and sustaining them, are millions of chemical reactions in your neural pathways. When the tradition says that God is the creator *ex nihilo,* it really means to affirm, some have said, that God creates each and every one of these ontological textures as if absolutely from nothing.

Creation from nothing does not describe a once-off action "at the beginning" of time, like the way in which we might knock over the first domino, where other dominos falling over are increasingly remote from the first action. God's creating and sustaining of every texture of reality — things, events, actions, thoughts — is as dramatically total and "from nothing" as God's original action in bringing about something rather than nothing. Everything that is hovers flickering in front of nothingness, saved from nothingness only by a constant and plenitudinous pouring forth of divine love and freedom, choosing that there be something rather than nothing, and that it be this thing. Remember from chapters two and three: the "being" of God is best understood as a verb. It is the be-ing of God, the action of God's being, that holds everything in existence; and not just every "thing" but every nuance, texture, and slice of the real, however one carves it up, into however many parts, from the most micro to the most cosmic.

Creation *ex nihilo* is, for the traditional theologian, quite lovely, but almost frightening: it can give a sense of dizzying vertigo in front of the abyss. It is the source of a notion of "participation," strong in classical Christianity, as God is so intimately active in every aspect of everything that is. From our point of view, the creation is almost an emanation of the being of God, as everything (and not just every "thing") within it is breathed out by the will of God, taking us close to some Neoplatonic conceptions. It is from God's point of view, though, that the creation is emphatically not a Neoplatonic emanation of the being of God, in that God does not need the creation to be fully and always God.

Creation *ex nihilo* then is one magnetic pole for thinking. Here is another one, also at the heart of classical Christianity. Human beings are created free. When the human being acts, it is not simply an emanation of the being of God, but is an action for which that human being is responsible. Between the human creature and God, there is a relationship, rather than an identity. Immediately we should see a certain tension between the first pole of thought, that God is the creator *ex nihilo,* the sustaining source not only of every being, but of every action of every being, and the second pole, that the human creature genuinely acts from her own integrity, where her action is in relation to God, and is not just a determined emanation of the being of God.

What are our options here? Well, we could resolve the tension by subordinating one pole to the other. This is precisely what does happen in the history of thought. We can insist that in fact God's action is the only real action in the universe, and that everything is a direct result of God's predetermined willing. Theologians such as Luther and Calvin are sometimes accused of thinking something like this. The position known as "occasionalism" explicitly insists that God is the only real source of action in the universe, affirming that God directly wills every event: when it seems to you that the gas stove heats the kettle, what happens is that God directly causes the water to boil on the same "occasion" that he directly causes the gas flame to be hot; hence the position is known as "occasionalism."

On the other hand, we can insist that with respect to our free actions,

God does not act, but withdraws so as to allow us to act without "interference." In this way we subordinate the pole of creation *ex nihilo* to the pole of thought that concerns human freedom. So, in an analysis of the ontological snapshot of the room you might be sitting in, we would in fact have two columns — one marked "directly the result of divine creative action" and the other "not the direct result of divine creative action." In the latter column would be all those actions that arise from our freedom. This account of human action, as being something that starts when God withdraws, is widely held, for example, in analytical philosophy of religion (or "analytical theology"), and also in the wider culture. It is, I think, what many people think relating to God is like, or would be like, if there were a God. God is like a very big and powerful agent. In this sense, divine and human action are a zero-sum game: the more divine action there is, the less space there is for the human. Rather like the relationship between a parent and a teenager, God must withdraw, if the human being is to be free. Strikingly, this is a premise shared by both atheists and many contemporary believers, and cuts across ecumenical and confessional lines.[1] Most significantly for us, the view that when humans act God must withdraw is also Kant's view, as I will go on to show. In fact, Kant's thinking this might well be a large part of why it is such a widespread cultural assumption, given the pervasiveness of Kant's influence on how we think about freedom.

One of the reasons for engaging in intellectual history must be this: it can help to make the ordinary seem strange, and to render the "obvious" fragile, by showing us that widespread presumptions are in fact extremely recent, or very local, or based on unfamiliar grounds. When we look at the conception of freedom in Western philosophy and theology, we learn that the zero-sum characterization of the relationship between divine and human freedom would be more or less universally rejected by the entire premodern tradition.[2] Modern thought, including much modern theol-

1. For critiques of the notion of concurrence, see the following: Thomas Flint, "Two Accounts of Providence," in *Divine and Human Action: Essays in the Metaphysics of Theism,* ed. Thomas V. Morris (Ithaca, NY: Cornell University Press, 1988); and William Hasker, "God the Creator of Good and Evil?" in *The God Who Acts: Philosophical and Theological Explorations,* ed. Thomas F. Tracy (University Park: Penn State University Press, 1994), pp. 137-46.

2. This point is made by Alfred J. Freddoso, "God's General Concurrence with Secondary Causes: Why Conservation Is Not Enough," *Philosophical Perspectives* 5 (1991): 553-85 (pp. 578-79); and by Kathryn Tanner, *God and Creation in Christian Theology: Tyranny or Empowerment?* (Minneapolis: Fortress, 2005).

ogy and philosophy of religion, has carried out a revolution, which for the most part has no monuments, and goes unrecorded. The revolution was so successful, that we do not even know that we are its children.

The premodern tradition, represented here by Aquinas, would insist on holding together the two poles of thought set out above, and saying both that the human being genuinely and freely acts, and is responsible for the action, and can do otherwise, but that God also acts directly and fully in this action. God's action "runs with" the action of the creature, it "concurs." This is "concurrence" or "concursus." Thinkers such as Aquinas and Suarez are clear about what is required for a proper account of concurrence:[3]

- God must act immediately and directly in the action of the creature.
- Neither God's action nor the creature's action would be by themselves sufficient for that action to occur.
- Neither action would exist in the absence of the other.

God, of course, could bring about the same effect acting by himself, but then it would not be by virtue of God's *concurring* action.

It is by no means straightforward to give a coherent account of divine concurrence. We have fairly uncomplicated analogies that can be derived or abstracted from experience for being the primary or sole cause of something, for things seeming to be causes that are not (a simulated image of a billiard ball hitting another billiard ball), and for indirect dependence (I need oxygen to breathe as a supporting condition for writing a book, but the oxygen is not directly a cause of my writing a book on Kant). It is less clear what we are asserting when we talk of the concurrence of God and our freedom. Some analogies are provided in the tradition, but in principle, and by definition, we know of nothing quite like it, because the relationship between God and the creature, between the creator *ex nihilo* and the created, is utterly unlike any relationship between creature and creature.

---

3. For my understanding of concurrence accounts, I am indebted to Alfred J. Freddoso, "Medieval Aristotelianism and the Case against Secondary Causation in Nature," in *Divine and Human Action: Essays in the Metaphysics of Theism,* ed. Thomas V. Morris (Ithaca, NY: Cornell University Press, 1988), pp. 74-118; "God's General Concurrence with Secondary Causes: Why Conversation Is Not Enough," *Philosophical Perspectives* 5 (1991): 553-85; and "God's General Concurrence with Secondary Causes: Pitfalls and Prospects," *American Catholic Philosophical Quarterly* 67 (1994): 131-56.

Most of our analogies for something like "concurrence" work by conceiving of a "split contribution to a single action." Typically, there are two favorite analogies. The first model works like this. You and I go outside and attempt to lift a car together; you are on the left, I am on the right. Let us say that neither one of us acting by ourselves can raise the car at all, but that together we can make it such that a bit of air appears between the wheels and the ground. In some ways, this seems to be a good analogy: it seems plausible to consider "lifting the car" a single action; neither action is sufficient by itself to perform the action; and my action of lifting the car would not occur at all were it not for your action of lifting the car. But then the analogy breaks down. On this model, there is still my distinct contribution, which I could make by myself, albeit unsuccessfully. For the analogy really to capture the rule that "God acts in our actions," it would need to be the case that you are acting in me, directly and immediately, even when I make a sole effort.

A second favored model is this: if I draw on a whiteboard with a marker, it seems plausible to say both that the marker causes the writing and that I cause the writing. In fact, Aquinas uses a similar analogy of a woodcutter wielding an axe. But again, the analogy is flawed; or, to put it another way, the analogy is, properly, only an analogy. Does the pen really "act"? Is it not just "used," so that it is part of the total action? In any case, there seems to be no space for anything like freedom in the case of the pen or the axe. Neither is ultimately responsible for its actions, nor can it do other than it does.

Furthermore, both models, the car-lifting and the marker on the whiteboard, come apart in that they fail to give an account of concurrence that is an *extra* texture of action, on top of creation *ex nihilo* and God's continual conservation of everything in face of threatening oblivion. Neither you on the left-hand corner of the car nor the pen would cease to exist if, for one moment, I ceased to will that you, or the pen, should exist. And this is what concurrence affirms. Concurrence is not an alternative to creation and God's action conserving the creation; it comes after these, as a more intense expression of what must be involved in creation *ex nihilo*.

It is important to understand that the drive toward concurrence does not primarily arise because of the sense that it is an uncomplicated, elegant, and non-mysterious model of causal influence. It is more that it is perceived as the only *theologically* appropriate model, which is compatible with the two poles of divine creativity and the distinctness and integrity of the creation. Concurrence, one of the mysteries of faith, is a contemplation on the claim, as put by David Burrell when reflecting on Aquinas, that "God not only causes each thing to be, and thus makes it able to act, but God also acts in its acting by causing it to be the cause that it is."[4] We have a shape within which our freedom must occur. Concurrence is not nonsense, it is not an apparition, or Swedenborgian flatulence. We can see perfectly clearly the different pressures on our thinking which have brought us to this point. We just cannot hold them all together. But our ability to hold things together is considered to be less important than the realization that the things that we are unable coherently to relate, as above with "freedom and equality," are indeed all somehow true, and true together. To know that we cannot hold them all together, without dropping any of them, is rationally satisfying: we know why we are doing it. But equally, doing this takes us beyond reason. Our reason, though, is a fairly paltry thing, and so our deep background cosmology and anthropology lead us to expect it to fail, and to need the lamplight of mystery to journey from mere intelligence to truth. "I see that you believe these things are true," Dante is told in purgatory, when contemplating God's mysterious action in human beings, "yet you do not see how. / Thus, though believed, their truth is hidden from you":

> You are like one who knows the name of a thing
> whose [nature], until it is explained
> by someone else, defies his understanding.
>
> (*Purgatorio*, Canto XX, lines 88-90)

Kant's Rejection of Concurrence

It is time now to move on to Kant's rejection of concurrence accounts. Here is a question. From what we know about Kant's mature account of what human freedom consists in, do we already know that he will reject concurrence accounts of divine and human action? It might seem that we do know this, if human beings must be ultimately responsible for their actions, and if they must be able to do otherwise. How could this be consistent with God acting in all our actions? But, in fact, this would be wrong.

---

4. David Burrell, *Freedom and Creation in Three Traditions* (Notre Dame, IN: University of Notre Dame Press, 1993), pp. 68-69. Burrell offers this as a paraphrase of Aquinas, *Summa Theologiae,* I. 105.2.

It is part of the tradition of thinking about concurrence to insist that God acting in all our actions is perfectly consistent with everything that Kant demands from freedom, that is, our being ultimately responsible for our actions, and our being able to do other than we do.

How can this work? Well, a partial answer is this. What we are really interested in when we ask whether persons are ultimately responsible, and whether they could have done otherwise, is whether they are somehow "externally" impacted by an "alien cause," something that comes from outside of themselves. The only "causes" that threaten our ultimate responsibility, and our ability to do otherwise, are these "external" causes. So we need to ask: what sorts of things are alien causes for the human being? Well, mechanistic deterministic chains of causation would be such things. Kant has removed these, by rendering them features of our reception of the world, rather than being in the world in itself. Other creatures, in particular other people, could be alien causes, if they force or coerce us in some way. Even our own desires and impulses can be alien causes, if they lead us away from what it is that we more fundamentally might want. So what sorts of things might be properly "internal" to the creature, in a way that does not threaten freedom? Perhaps my own character, where I broadly approve and esteem myself; or my own sense of a worthwhile project; or my adoption of a set of fundamental principles. If my action is according to my principles, which are embedded in my character, this sort of "causation" does not seem to threaten freedom.

Here is the question: what about God? Is God an external or an internal cause to the creature? The answer given by the premodern tradition, and by Aquinas, is that God is emphatically an internal cause. Consider: God brings the creature into being from nothing; God sustains the creature constantly in existence in the face of oblivion; the essence of human nature is a part of the uncreated divine understanding, and so the being of God provides the very "what-it-is-ness" of the creature; and God is the final end and purpose for which all creatures are created. How could God's action upon the creature ever be "external"? God is, in fact, more "internal" to the creature than the creature is to itself. God, as "be-ing," a constantly plenitudinous action, is intimately at the center of all beings.

This shows that we do not know that Kant has rejected concurrence just because Kant wants us to be ultimately responsible for our actions, and to be able to do otherwise. But reject concurrence he does. We know this because he tells us. A few representative texts give a flavor of Kant's departure from the tradition on this point:

. . . there takes place no *concursus* of God with natural occurrences. For just because they are supposed to be natural occurrences, it is presupposed already that their first proximate cause is in nature itself, and it must be sufficient to effect the occurrence, even if the cause itself (like every natural cause) is grounded in God as the supreme cause. (*LPR*, 28: 1106)

Thus God cannot concur in the causality of freely acting beings toward his moral ends in the world, for he must not be regarded as *causa* of their free actions. That which gives free actions the *complementum ad sufficientam* toward divine moral ends (holiness) is the spirit of God. This, however, if the actions are still to remain imputable, must also not be *causata* of the holy spirit, but only the removal of obstacles to freedom. (*R*, 6167; 18: 473-74)

But as for the concept, customary in the schools, of divine *intervention* or collaboration *(concursus)* toward an effect in the sensible world, this must be given up. For to want to pair what is disparate and to let what is itself the complete cause of alterations in the world *supplement* its own predetermining providence (which must therefore have been inadequate) during the course of the world is, *first*, self-contradictory. (*PP*, 8: 362)[5]

It is not permitted to think of God's concursus with free actions. These actions are events in the world. If God is the determining cause of these actions, they are not free. But God however does not concur; then he would not be a solitary cause. If I say, God concurs with the determination of our wills, then that would be again a miracle. If God concurs with morality, then the human being has no moral worth, because nothing can be imputed to him. (*DR*, 28: 1309)[6]

---

5. I depart here from the translation in the Cambridge Edition, which translates "*gebräuchlich in den Schulen*" as "current in the academic world"; *gebräuchlich* can mean not just "current" but "customary" or "usual," and *die Schulen* should be permitted to have the connotation of the medieval Schools (of the scholastic theologians), as well as the systems of the German rationalists. As well as being justified in its own right, the revised translation makes more sense; the position Kant is opposing is much older, as he would know, than a "current" theory in his "academic world."

6. My translation.

These few passages are representative samples only: there are many more similar texts from Kant's writings in the 1780s and 1790s (see *R*, 4748, 5632, 6019, 6118, 6121, 6167, 6169, 6171, 8083; *NTV*, 28: 1207-13; *MK₂*, 28: 811; *ML₁* 28: 347; *MD*, 28: 648). As with Kant's claim that God does not (directly) create space and time, I have found that Kant scholars can become distressed at the suggestion that Kant would trouble himself with a scholastic theological matter such as concurrence, even in the process of denying it. Again the response has to be Kant's texts themselves. Whatever we think about it, Kant simply does engage with the question of concurrence, and takes the time, on a number of occasions, in lectures, reflections, and published works, to deny concurrence accounts of divine and human action. Our task is to understand these texts, not to doubt their existence because of a prior conception of what sort of thing the mature Kant ought to think about.

  The picture that Kant settles on is this: God is the creator *ex nihilo* of noumenal substances, that is, of substances as they really are, independent of our spatial and temporal reception. Kant considers, in a traditional way, that God must constantly will to sustain these substances in existence. But the actions of substances are not the direct creative products of the action of God. We have, in fact, already seen Kant's denial of concurrence at work in one of the passages quoted in the previous chapter. Remember this:

> Thus space is nothing in itself and is not a thing as a divine work, but rather lies in us and can only obtain in us. . . . (*R*, 6057; 18: 439)

The traditional theologian would not say this, *even if* he or she agreed with Kant that space and time are features of the way in which we receive the world, rather than being in the world as it is in itself. What the traditional theologian would say is this: space is a divine work, as a divinely created feature of the way in which we receive the world. In the ontological snapshot of the room, one of the "non-thing-like" things captured would be our reception of the world in spatial and temporal terms, where this reception constantly depends upon creative divine action. The reason Kant says that space is not a divine work is directly related to his denial of concurrence: space and time are (involuntary) products of the human noumenal action of receiving the world. And, as we have seen, where we act, God does not act. Otherwise, it would not be our action, as God is conceived as in some sense an "external" cause. For Kant, anything that is a product of our action, whether free or unfree, is not directly a product of divine creativity, and belongs in the column of things "not directly created by God." This is explicitly what Kant writes, as the larger context of the quotation emphatically shows:

> Appearances are not actually creations, thus neither is the [phenomenal] human being; rather he is merely the appearance of a divine creation. His condition of acting and being acted upon is an appearance and depends on him. The human being is the *principium originarium* [originating principle] of appearances. (*R*, 6057; 18: 439)

I have not attempted in this chapter to offer a proof of the truth of concurrence accounts of divine and human freedom. If anything, a meditation on concurrence will draw our attention instead to some of the beneficially darkening consequences of thinking about freedom in terms of concurrence. Throughout our discussion, what has been the problem with freedom? Well, the problem is always, how is it used? Just to be free for freedom's sake opens us up to a pointless ability to destroy ourselves and others. Sheer freedom, for no purpose, is a restless energy waiting for a character, a cause, a project. We desire, for our freedom to flourish, to somehow be led in the dance, for our freedom to be turned to a cause, a project, a purpose. The history of human folly is the evening's dance card of chosen partners: nations, empires, science, fascism, communism, capitalism, democracy, history, progress, romance, self-expression, obedience, and, of course, freedom itself, taken as an end in itself. All of these have been variously called upon to substitute for the traditional concept of God in philosophy since Kant. We will even see, in the next chapter, that Kant himself, in his later years, begins to tip over into a hope in our own "divinity," manifested, perhaps, by a progress in history.

The traditional theologian will always have profound reservations here, insisting that only God could ever be the whole, entire, and all-sufficient resting place, and satiation, of all that we want from our freedom. This is what concurrence accounts of divine and human freedom draw attention to: that there is only one cause, only one principle, and only one will, who can be trusted never to be violent, external, and alien to our true freedom. This is God: transcendent, unknowable, ungraspable, but also intimately present in the creation and in our every action. Now, of course, "God" and "transcendence" can be used to buttress the most violent of all human ideologies. The tradition calls such uses of "God" idolatry, and human religious activity threatens constantly to tip over into it. Presented with the threat of idolatry, the theologian will want to draw attention to the way in which transcendence does not necessarily enter thinking as a presence or a foundation. When properly understood its role can be precisely the opposite: to provide a constant pedal-note under all our endeavors, which tells us that we are only partially grasping a fragment of the plenitude of truth. Transcendence enters the system as an absence, a darkness, a question mark, and a sign of our humility and createdness. Here, perhaps, the traditional theologian and the more rigorous sort of atheist could sing the same litany: if God is dead, let there be no other gods. Only God can be God, even if there is no God.

Conclusion

Kant, I have argued, does believe in God. The rupture and challenge that Kant's thought marks in relation to the tradition is not on this issue. The greatest challenge is not belief in God, but Kant's belief about how God acts in relation to God's creatures and, in particular, the relation between divine action and human freedom. We have now seen enough to understand why Kant will struggle with traditional readings of so many Christian doctrines, all of which require in some sense a concurrence account of divine action and human freedom in order to begin to run: for example, incarnation (a divine and human nature in one person); and grace and atonement (whereby God acts in us, when we cannot perform the action ourselves). Our central interest is in the question of freedom. We have reflected upon one of faith's mysteries in relation to human freedom: that God can act in our actions without violating our freedom, even such significant freedom that the mature Kant desires. Kant accepts much that can be found in a broad tradition of Christian Platonism. But, importantly and dramatically, he rejects concurrence, and this rejection, I have suggested, lies at the heart of two things: first of all, the difference between modern and premodern conceptions of human freedom; and second, the reason Kant cannot manage to turn his Christianized Platonism into Christian Platonism. In the next and final chapter, we will see the impact of Kant's rejection of concurrence. I suggest that Kant's inability to accept concurrence accounts leads ultimately to the tearing apart of his system, as the demands of freedom render the hope for the highest good ultimately impossible, or at least, impossible for God to achieve while God is something distinct from us and our reason.

CHAPTER EIGHT

Becoming Divine:
Autonomy and the Beatific Vision

I have already asked you, in chapter four, to take an imaginary stroll to Kant's grave, in present-day Kaliningrad, where the tombstone is marked with the epitaph:

> Two things fill the mind with ever new and increasing admiration and reverence, the more often and more steadily one reflects on them: *the starry heavens above me and the moral law within me.*

Kant's grave, I commented, has become a sort of shrine for newlyweds. We are now going to visit the same graveyard, but more than two hundred years earlier, on a frozen morning in February 1804. It is Kant's funeral. There is a large crowd, much larger than his small circle of personal friends was expecting. One of Kant's closest and oldest friends, Johann Georg Scheffner, is among the mourners as Kant's coffin is lowered into the ground. As I reported in the second chapter, after the funeral Scheffner wrote in a letter that "you will not believe the kind of tremor that shook my existence when the first frozen clumps of earth were thrown on his coffin — my head and heart still tremble."[1] This reaction has been ascribed to Scheffner's awareness that although Kant, in his philosophy, had "held out for eternal life and a future state," in the forum of his own heart and mind he had become "cold to such ideas."[2] We also heard, in chapter two,

---

1. Manfred Kuehn, *Kant: A Biography* (Cambridge: Cambridge University Press, 2001), p. 2; the reference is Scheffner to Lüdeck, March 5, 1804, in *Briefe von und an Scheffner*, 5 vols., ed. Arthur Warda and Carl Driesche (Munich and Leipzig: Duncker and Humblot, 1916), 2: 443.
2. Kuehn, *Kant: A Biography*, p. 3.

that another friend of Kant in old age, Karl Ludwig Pörschke, reported of the philosopher that "he often assured me even when he had been *Magister* for a long time, he did not doubt any dogma *(Satz)* of Christianity. Little by little, one after the other, they broke off."[3] Another of Kant's friends, Johann Friedrich Abegg, wrote that by the end of his life Kant really thought, "Believe nothing, hope for nothing! Do your duty here."[4]

The impression formed by Kant's friends receives some confirmation — although, I will argue, only partially — from Kant's very last writings, a fragmented collection of meditations gathered together and published posthumously under the title *Opus Postumum*. In writings from the early 1800s, in Kant's darkening twilight years, we find the same two questions reiterated:

What is God? (*OP,* 21: 9, 13)

and:

Is there a God? (*OP,* 21: 9, 13, 17, 23)

Strikingly, Kant writes that the question "is there a God?" is a problem that "still remains unresolved" (*OP,* 21: 17).

This should strike us as strange, or at least as a shift, given the journey we have taken with Kant so far. We began this journey, in chapter two, by contemplating Kant's claim from the mid-1780s that God "is the true abyss for human reason." We recall Kant's words:

One can neither resist nor tolerate the thought of a being represented as the highest of all possible things, which may say to itself, "I am from eternity to eternity, and outside me there is nothing except what exists through my will." (*LPR,* 28: 1033)

We have seen that from the 1750s to the 1790s Kant fully means and feels the impossibility of both resisting the idea of God and of tolerating it. The early Kant is convinced that there must be a God, in whose divine understanding are to be found the uncreated essences of all things, from

3. Kuehn, *Biography,* p. 138; the reference is Johann Friedrich Abegg, *Reisetagebuch von 1798* (Frankfurt: Insel Verlag, 1976), p. 184.

4. Kuehn, *Biography,* p. 392; the reference is to Abegg, *Reisetagebuch,* p. 184.

which God chooses to create. God then chooses to place these created substances in relation with each other, generating the whole experienced realm of space, time, and causation. In Kant's early thought, "freedom" simply involves doing what you want, even if what you want is determined by mechanical chains of causation. But this God, essential to ground the created universe, increasingly becomes a millstone for Kant when thinking about human freedom, as Kant reaches for a more ambitious conception of this freedom. Kant is convinced that if God is the source of space, time, and causation, then we cannot be free, as we will be locked into patterns of mechanical cause and effect. This is the problem that we left Kant with at the end of the fourth chapter.

Such a God is difficult to tolerate. As we saw in chapter five, Kant achieves a resolution by finding that space and time, and the consequent mechanical and deterministic patterns of causation, are not features of the universe created by God, but are features of our reception of the universe. This opens up the possibility, at least, that the universe as it really is, independent of our reception of it, is amenable to freedom. It is possible that behind the spatial and temporal appearances that make up our experience, there is a universe of noumenal substances, unconstrained by space and time, and so not determined by mechanical causation. We cannot *know* about such noumenal substances, but practical reason, ordered toward the good, is required to form beliefs about their reality. Belief in God is at least rendered "tolerable" in that God does not constrict and undermine our freedom by being the all-powerful source of chains of determining causation. God, in a sense, Kant tells us, is not the creator of space and time, or of appearances.

Given all the difficulty that Kant has with his "intolerable" God, would it not be better to drop the concept altogether? Well, Kant does not, and this leads us to the second part of the quotation from the mid-1780s, that belief in God cannot be "resisted." God, for Kant, is indeed a nuisance when thinking about our freedom, our ability to do other than the good, and our ultimate responsibility for our actions. But freedom in this sense is not, for Kant, the most important thing. Of more importance is what our freedom is *for:* and this is the highest good, where we become what it is that we ought to be, fully realizing our rational nature, which leads, as a consequence, to harmony, community, and happiness. Practical reason tells us that at the end of all our striving, and as a consequence of it, there ought to be harmony, community, and happiness. Now, is it in fact the case that our moral efforts, such as they are, lead to harmony, community, and happiness? Manifestly not. Who or what can guarantee that the universe will unfold as it ought to, such that we perfectly express our rational nature, and achieve autonomy? Kant's answer, at least throughout the 1780s and 1790s, is "God." God, an intolerable problem when thinking about freedom, is an irresistible source of consolation and hope when thinking about the highest good.

In the writings from the last years of his life, as Kant circles the foothills of extinction, he launches a rather different account of what sort of reality God might have from any we find in his early or mature thought. In the *Opus Postumum* Kant keeps returning to the same answer to these two questions, "what is God?" and "is there a God?" The reality of the concept of God, Kant writes, is to be found "in the mind of man," as a "principle of moral-practical reason" (*OP*, 22: 121). Although in this sense, "there exists a God" (*OP*, 22: 122), God is simply the "principle" of moral law-giving (*OP*, 22: 122). We find God wherever moral-practical reasoning is at work, or as Kant writes, wherever we put "freedom under the law [of reason]," and make this "the ground of the determination of one's actions," such that one's duties are also one's commands:

> The idea of such a being, before whom all knees bow, etc., emerges from this imperative and not the reverse, and a God is thought necessarily, subjectively, in human practical reason, although not given objectively. (*OP*, 22: 121)

We no longer have the assurances of the second *Critique* that practical reason postulates "the objective reality" of God, whereby even "the theoretical cognition of pure reason" receives, as Kant puts it, an "increment," albeit through practical reason (*CPrR*, 5: 134). Now, Kant writes that God is not a "*substance* outside myself, whose existence I postulate as a hypothetical being" (*OP*, 22: 123). Rather "I, man, am this being myself — it is not some substance outside me" (*OP*, 21: 25). Take note, "I, man, am this being myself," where this being is "God"; "I," man, am God myself, inasmuch as I am capable of giving myself a moral law. Our own commanding of the moral law to ourselves, or as Kant describes it, "the spirit of man, under a compulsion which is only possible through *freedom*" (*OP*, 21: 25), itself has the mark of divinity. From this divine activity "emerges" "a God" thought "in human practical reason." Kant writes that while "all expressions of moral-practical reason are divine," in that they "contain the moral imperative," "it is not God in substance whose existence is proved"

(*OP*, 21: 26). Kant tells us that "the commanding subject," the free human subject, "is God," where "this commanding being is not outside man as a substance different from man" (*OP*, 21: 22).

Two things, I would argue, should leap out at us from these passages. First of all, I think it has to be admitted that Kant no longer believes in God, as a being outside of us, with a reality independent of our moral endeavors. So is Kant an atheist, or a secularist? Well, perhaps a sort of atheist, in that he no longer believes in the rationalist God of his early and mature thought; but it is harder to say that Kant is a secularist, if by that we mean someone who wants to strip away references to the divine or the transcendent in the interests of scientific naturalism or neutral rationality. And this is the second thing we should notice. Kant expresses his shift away from his Christianized Platonism in highly religious terms, explaining that we are divine, insofar as we give the moral law to ourselves. The traditional theological concept of theosis involves the human being becoming divine by virtue of divine action and participation in the Godhead. Kant's final reflections curiously parallel a sort of theosis, except with an important difference. We become divine, but by virtue of our own action, and by virtue of our participation in the moral law. We have a sort of theosis whereby as we become divine, God is eclipsed and vanishes, or dissolves into us.

The remainder of this chapter will consist of two parts. In the first part, I will seek to understand what might have happened in Kant's thinking, to take him from his mature belief in God, on the basis of practical reason, to his very final rejection of belief in God. I suggest that a theologian looking at Kant's mature thought, at the height of his Christianized Platonism, could in fact expect that things will unfold precisely as they do for Kant. The theologian might even commend Kant's perspicuity and, as ever with Kant, his intellectual honesty and self-interrogation, while disagreeing with Kant's starting point. Where we need to go, to see this, is to the heart of Kant's conception of autonomy, in relation to his concept of freedom. Although Kant claims in the 1780s that only God can guarantee that we can achieve the highest good, we will see that when the theologian looks at what Kant says about autonomy, she will see, as Kant comes to see, that there is not much that God can really do for us, *given* what Kant says about human freedom. And what Kant says about human freedom, as we saw in the previous chapter, was that when the human being acts, God cannot act, and so we must achieve autonomy alone.

I will suggest that Kant's final movement away from belief in God, toward an account of our own reason as divine, expresses a deep insight into the direction a religious worldview might need to go, when contemplation of, and participation in, God is no longer the beginning and end of our perfection, but where freely willing in community with other equal and non-determined beings is the height of human perfection.

In the second part of the chapter, I will allow the religious but non-Christian Kant and the theologian to speak to each other. Avoiding some of the more predictable brickbats and name-calling, I will seek out what might be the most profound unease that the Christian Platonist would feel about his cousin, the Christianized Platonist, when standing under and contemplating Kant's position. This will lead us into fundamental theology, and the doctrine of God, and the question of what human freedom is in relation to God. In turn, this will lead us to reflect upon the perennial encounter between theology, as a reflection upon revelation and mystery, and philosophy, as the human seeking of wisdom through reason. In Kant, I will suggest, we find a philosopher, in the most ambitious, classical, and visionary sense, engaging the categories of theology with a self-disciplined reticence, which the theologian will, in part, regret, but also, in a sense, admire and appreciate.

The Shift to the *Opus Postumum*

First of all, we look into the question of how Kant has shifted from his mature position on God, to his late, dying position. One way of reading the *Opus Postumum* would lead us to an exclusively biographical, almost "medical" explanation, in terms of Kant's failing powers of reasoning. The *Opus Postumum* is a strange text: repetitive, assertive, enigmatic, disordered, and interwoven with notes about what to have for dinner, alongside mildly hypochondriac theories about health and diet. By all accounts, Kant's powers of reasoning declined steadily, but significantly, over at least six years, from the late 1790s until his death in 1804.

The distinguished anatomist and surgeon Theodor Meckel (1756-1803) visited Kant in 1797, but reported that Kant's reasoning powers had so declined that the old philosopher could make no further contribution.[5] Kant's friend Abegg commented that "Kant does not read his own writings any longer; does not right away understand what he has written himself

---

5. Kuehn, *Biography*, p. 390.

before . . . [and] his weakness is that he repeats everything that he is told."[6] Kant himself is reported to have declared the writings that make up the *Opus Postumum* to be "his chief work . . . which represents his system as a completed whole,"[7] but this was received by Kant's circle as further evidence of his declining judgment. About "the last scribblings over which Kant died," Kant's acquaintance Christian Jacob Kraus writes, "no sense or understanding wants to enter into them."[8] Kant is now an old man.

There is a sadness, a human poignancy, about his final years, the last flickering phenomenal eighteenth- and (briefly) nineteenth-century appearances of the eternal noumenal Kant. Still taking his regular daily walk, he now uses a slow, deliberate, flat-footed stomp, in the belief that this will help to prevent him falling, which it does not.[9] He squabbles like a toddler with friends, who are concerned that Kant's diet has become restricted to sandwiches made with grated English cheddar cheese: "He insisted excitedly on the satisfaction of his craving," writes Ehregott Wasianski:

> This was the first time I noticed a certain kind of animosity against me, which was meant to suggest that I had stepped over the line he had drawn for me. He appealed to the fact that this food had never harmed him and could not harm him. He ate the cheese — and more had to be grated. I had to be silent and give in, after having tried everything to change his mind.[10]

Wasianski finally won the argument about cheese when Kant lost consciousness the next morning while being taken on a walk through his house by his sister.[11] By report, Kant had difficulty remembering words such as "bedroom," and would eject eccentric theories about cats being peculiarly "electrical" animals, or beer (but not wine or spirits) being a slow-acting poison.[12] "Kant the great thinker," his friend wrote, "now stopped thinking."[13]

For the theologian, there is perhaps a delicious and cheap temptation

6. Kuehn, *Biography,* p. 391.
7. Kuehn, *Biography,* pp. 409-10.
8. Kuehn, *Biography,* p. 410.
9. Kuehn, *Biography,* p. 415.
10. Kuehn, *Biography,* p. 420.
11. Kuehn, *Biography,* p. 420.
12. Kuehn, *Biography,* p. 416.
13. Kuehn, *Biography,* p. 416.

to argue that Kant's loss of belief in God can be put down to his declining powers of reasoning. Our *Zeitgeist* rarely throws up invitations to describe atheism as a symptom of dementia, or, possibly, of repeated small strokes. But the invitation should be declined. When it comes to Kant's dying thoughts about God, I think the most accurate thing to say is that Kant is indeed losing some of his powers, but not perhaps his insight. Rather, Kant is losing his mental strength to resist, as he previously could manage, the inner momentum of some of his central philosophical conceptions. Even in his prime, Kant was physically weak. But intellectually he was a Hercules. At the height of his powers we might say, perhaps, that Kant used this strength to hold back the momentum of his own ideas. He has now lost this strength, and his own thinking floods over him. Such a view fits with a more sympathetic account of his final years from his friend Pörschke, who refuted the suggestion that "Kant's mind is already dead," writing that

> To be sure, he is no longer capable of extended and concentrated thought; he now lives largely from the rich store of his memory, but even now he makes exceptional combinations and projects.[14]

Or we would go further, perhaps, and say that Kant has exceptional breakdowns in his thinking, and that just as his intellectual efforts were supremely illuminating, so too is his intellectual collapse.

To understand this claim we need, finally, to go to the heart of one of the most contested areas of Kant interpretation. What, precisely, at the height of his powers in the 1780s and 1790s, does Kant mean by autonomy, whereby we give ourselves *(autos)* the moral law *(nomos)?*

Autonomy

When Kant talks about the highest good, part of what he means is that we become "autonomous." What is it then to be "autonomous"? It is to give ourselves the moral law, the law about what ought to be done. What is the moral law? Well, the moral law is that which can be willed by all rational beings as a law, for themselves and for all other rational beings. Fine: but what *is that?* What sort of thing, for example, can be willed by all rational beings? To know this, we have to know something about the sort of being

14. Kuehn, *Biography,* p. 390.

that we are dealing with when we talk about a "rational being." Where are rational beings to be found? That is to say, beings who are capable of acting for reasons, rather than being determined by spatial and temporal patterns of deterministic causation?

We know that such beings are not to be found in the realm of spatial and temporal appearances, because such appearances are merely the phenomena ("that which appears") of a more fundamental reality. The moral law, and our true moral motivation for following the moral law, *never* appear in space and time. If we were to ask upon what morality is based, or what the supreme principle of morality is, we know, if we have followed Kant, that it will not be in our empirical nature, in our desires, in good empirical consequences, in feelings of happiness or benevolence. We will not find the principle of morality in these things — not because Kant has something "against" consequences or happiness or benevolence, but because these attempts to ground morality all attempt to locate it in the empirical realm of appearances. When Kant dismisses "empirical happiness" as the ground of morality, it is more the "empirical" part of the conjunct that he objects to, rather than happiness. This works across the board, and undercuts standard accounts of Kant as uninterested in consequences, or virtue, or character, or desire, or happiness. When searching for the supreme principle of morality, for the core of morality, and only then, Kant is indeed uninterested in empirical manifestations of consequences, virtue, character, happiness, desire, because these are all mere phenomenal appearances. Hence, infamously, Kant declares in the *Groundwork* that when looking for the foundations of moral philosophy, our search must be "cleansed of everything that may be only empirical and that belongs to anthropology" (*GW*, 4: 389). All empirical manifestations are merely determined features of how we receive what is fundamentally going on at the level of noumenal reality. Kant is interested, though, in ultimate happiness, and consequences at the level of our noumenal selves.

The true "rational beings," whose universal consent we would have to discern when looking for what all rational beings can will, are in fact the noumenal non-spatial and non-temporal selves that underlie appearances.[15] So in the *Groundwork,* Kant writes that the law that is valid for us is that which arises from "our proper self," which is "our will as intelligence," and

---

15. In identifying our rational selves with our noumenal selves, I align myself here with Karl Ameriks, "Vindicating Autonomy: Kant, Sartre, and O'Neill," in *Kant and Moral Autonomy,* ed. Oliver Sensen (Cambridge: Cambridge University Press, 2013), pp. 53-70.

not "*what belongs to mere appearance*" (*GW,* 4: 461). We would need to know what these noumenal beings will. What is it to "will something"? It is to set an end for ourselves. So what we need to know is which ends noumenal beings could set for themselves. That is to say, we need to know which ends such rational beings could set, without violating their own nature. Noumenal beings are not impeded by deterministic chains of causation or by sensuous appetites, and are not coerced by any other creature, or even by the uncreated God. But they are intrinsically shaped by reason itself, conforming to the demands of reason, which are not external demands, because they express the deep down essential nature of noumenal selves. In this, they resemble the rationalist conception of God set out in chapters two and three: it in no way violates the freedom of the divine will to be "shaped" by reason, as reason is entirely internal to the nature of God. So too for us. Later thinkers, and even contemporaries of Kant, such as Fichte, were quick to disagree, and to find that even "reason" is an external and binding constraint on the free human subject, unleashing a torrent of relativism and romantic self-expression. But this is not Kant's view. Reason is never an extrinsic and alien cause for us. We would know that if an end is somehow in violation of our essential nature, which is reason, then such an end could not be rationally willed by noumenal beings. Whether or not an end violates our essential nature, which is reason, is a deep and reliable test of whether we are truly acting autonomously, and giving to ourselves something that is indeed the moral law.

Now we reach a characteristically Kantian loop, which some find profound, and others, in the end, viciously circular. We can join the loop by asking "what is reason?" The answer is that reason is "that which can be willed by all reasonable (noumenal and free) beings." Fine, but what is this? Well, it is that which expresses the deep and essential nature of such beings. So, what is the deep and essential nature of such beings? Well, it is reason itself. And now, it seems, we go around the roundabout again, in an eternal right-hand lane. "What is reason?" Well, it is "that which can be willed by all reasonable (noumenal and free) beings." And so on.

In fact, Kant does have an exit ramp (or slip-road) that takes him off the roundabout, but he is not a very clear navigator. Like all poor navigators, he does not always tell us what we need to know at the moment we need it. What we need is something that breaks out of the circle whereby "being universally willed" equals "being reasonable," which equals "being universally willed." Where we find the escape-route is in Kant's mature account of what "reason" is. What ultimately is reason? It is the ability to set an end *at all,* where by "setting an end" I make something my project *because I have chosen it for a reason,* rather than it being determined by something else. So Kant writes, "rational nature is distinguished from the rest of nature by this, that it sets itself an end," the value of which can be "abstracted" from the question of which "end" is "to be *effected,*" the "attainment of this or that end" (*GW,* 4: 437).

So, can we do whatever we want, as long as we set "an end"? Emphatically, we cannot. That which a noumenal being cannot rationally do is this: intend to violate the project of end-setting as such (abstracted from the consideration of particular ends). The project of end-setting is valuable, not because it is *my project,* but because it is the essential nature of reason as such, and the essence of every noumenal being is to be constituted by reason. The rational noumenal self will value the project and activity of end-setting as such. The rational noumenal self will seek to realize those ends, its own and the ends of others, that are compatible with all rational noumenal selves realizing their ends. Some ends are incompatible with other end-setters also having ends, and these in a proper sense "violate" our nature and "contradict" reason. We do wrong, then, when we deny the ability of ourselves, or of others, to set their own ends, and when we fail to realize ends that are compatible with the ability of others to do the same. Reason, the activity of end-setting, is valuable in itself. This intrinsic value is contagious to any being who engages in the activity of end-setting: if the activity of end-setting is intrinsically valuable, the source of end-setting, the end-setters, or we would say "persons," have value in themselves. From this arises a celebrated feature of Kant's moral philosophy, that every "rational being *exists* as an end in itself, *not merely as a means* to be used by this or that will at its discretion" (*GW,* 4: 428). Kant calls the moral community where noumenal selves value the project and activity of end-setting the "kingdom of ends." He writes that "in this way a world of rational beings *(intelligible world)* as a kingdom of ends is possible, through the giving of their own laws by all persons as members" (*GW,* 4: 438).

Is, then, the problem solved? It hardly seems that it is. Although Kant's account is no longer straightforwardly circular, it does not look particularly informative. How could it be, when the true moral agents whose end-setting we need to consult are our noumenal selves, who are in principle impossible to experience in space and time? Practical reason allows us to postulate that we are free noumenal selves, but it gives us no substantive knowledge about ourselves. Kant might have told us what the supreme principle of morality is: that which can be universalized by all end-setters

prob SK – memo: PLATO

who value end-setting as such, and not because it is their end-setting, or this particular end. But has Kant given us some examples, at least, of the sort of thing that the supreme principle of morality leads us to adopt, as a guideline for concrete ethical action, or practical policy? It does not seem that he has.

Is this lack of concreteness a problem for an attempt to set out a "supreme principle of morality"? At the very least, we must admit that the lack of determinate content has generated the obsessive but hardly lucrative industry of agonizing about Kant's various formulas for deriving universal laws. Nonetheless, I want to spend a few paragraphs giving Kant two cheers for being so unhelpful about specifics. Compare Kant's account with what we might call Aquinas's "supreme principle" for morality, that "good is to be done, and evil avoided." As with Kant, this tells us what constitutes the right thing to do (it involves ensuring that good should flourish), but hardly what sort of thing might be right. Similarly, the tradition of utilitarianism tells us that we should maximize happiness, but we have to do all the work of saying what happiness actually is. Virtue ethics tells us that the right action is that which contributes to a virtuous character, but again, all the work has yet to be done in discerning what a virtuous character actually consists in. In all these cases, when dealing with the "supreme principles" of morality (God, the good, happiness, virtue), we have to do the hard work of interpretation and application before we get to any specific content. Kant's supreme principle (rational end-setting) will need much interpretation and application, and this is indeed what Kant undertakes to do in a range of work, especially in the 1790s.

We have already seen that rationalists, and Platonists more widely, are concerned with the ways in which fundamental reality makes its appearance in the phenomenal realm. Kant, with rationalist and Platonic strands in his work, is no exception. In lectures on anthropology, and in work on applied ethics in the 1790s, Kant shows himself to be entirely absorbed in the study of the textures by which our underlying noumenal moral disposition manifests itself in the phenomenal realm. In lesser-known works, Kant writes extensively about childhood moral formation, the cultivation of virtue over time, theories of education, and the process of moral struggle and character-building; he also expresses psychological interest in feelings of awe and respect for morality, and our appropriate satisfaction in our attempt to follow the moral law. That Kant is fascinated with these appearances cannot be taken as evidence, although some have tried, that he is no longer committed to the underlying noumenal reality. As we have seen, again and again, we would *expect* Platonists to be intrigued by appearances, while insisting that appearances could be quite different from the underlying reality from which they fundamentally derive.

At this point, we can see how Kant's *Groundwork* can be read, provocatively but suggestively, as a faithful variant upon a perennial Platonic discipline of spiritual exercises, whereby we perform a type of *askesis,* stripping the self of false consolations and distorting passions, as we aspire toward a form of rational self-transcendence. Through the exercise of reason, we purify our will and intelligence of passions, distractions, and obsessions. The aspiration is to transcend the self, and to join a harmonious community with other rational agents and with the cosmos as a whole. Perhaps we do not find in the *Groundwork* specific injunctions, because it is an attempt to orient and transform us toward the self-transcendence that comes about through participating in universal reason as such, in that which is, as Kant puts it, "good without limitation" (*GW* I, 4: 394).

If we were to look for the living heart of Kant's theological rationalism, understood as a spiritual discipline, this comparison with Platonic exercises of self-transcendence is where we might at least begin. It would provide common ground between Kant's refusal to identify that which is "good without limit" with anything penultimate, and a tradition of Christian spirituality which refuses to find its resting point in anything conditioned or limited. In the context of asking what is "good without limitation" Kant rejects whole swathes of created reality: sensuous inclinations (*GW* I, 4: 403); all the gifts of fortune such as "power, riches, honor, even health and . . . complete wellbeing and satisfaction" (*GW* I, 4: 393); "*talents* of mind," such as "understanding, wit, judgment," and "qualities of *temperament,*" such as "courage, resolution, perseverance in one's plans" (*GW* I, 4: 393), including "moderation in affects and passions, self-control, and calm reflection" (*GW* I, 4: 394).

There is a sense in which Kant is in broad and deep agreement with a Platonic Christian tradition, when we remember that Kant is not giving a list of everything that is good to a degree, and for some purposes, but rather, that he is searching for that which can be declared "good without limitation." Aquinas also denies unconditioned worth to a similar range of penultimate goods: all the "goods of fortune,"[16] the "goods of the body,"[17]

---

16. Aquinas, *Summa Contra Gentiles,* III. 1, 30-31.
17. Aquinas, *Summa Contra Gentiles,* III. 1, 32.1.

and all moral virtues ordered to particular aspects of human flourishing.[18] When presented with an ascent to the unconditioned, with Platonic strains, it is important always to hold in mind that penultimate goods need not be regarded as unimportant as such, and certainly not as pernicious. Rather, the point is that they do not have the unlimited and unconditioned importance of being our final and all-satiating resting place.

I am content to allow the comparison between Platonic spiritual exercises and the recommendations of the *Groundwork* to be no more than loose and suggestive. For the purposes of my wider argument, nothing particularly hangs upon it. Nonetheless, the suggestion deserves further reflection, and cannot be ruled out as fanciful. Kant himself praises Plato for finding "his ideas preeminently in everything that is practical" (A 314-15/B 271-72), which involves ascending and abstracting from all particular examples and "possible objects of experience" until we attain the "archetype" of "moral perfection," even though "obstacles in human nature" may "hold us at a distance from it" (A 314-15/B 271-72). Kant insists, for example, that any philosopher "would do well" to "pursue" the idea of the "Platonic republic." Kant explains that the "Platonic republic" is a "necessary idea," abstracted from "present obstacles" which arise "from neglect of the true ideas in the giving of laws" (A 316/B 373). Such an ideal points to an arrangement where "the greatest human freedom" is provided "according to laws that permit the freedom of each to exist together with that of others" (A 316/B 373). From such an arrangement, as we have come to expect, Kant explains that "happiness" would "follow of itself," without being the explicit goal (A 316/B 373).

The suggestive evidence becomes stronger when one considers Kant's own reflections on pedagogy, given in lectures in 1776-77, 1780, 1783-84, and 1786-87. Kant reflects that education should be ordered neither to the ends of the "home" nor the "state," but rather toward the "formation" of the "personality," and the "perfection to which humanity is destined," where "the germs which lie in the human being" must be "developed further and further" (*LPed*, 9: 448). Education should "pay attention to *moralization*," whereby we "acquire the disposition to choose nothing but good ends . . . which are necessarily approved by everyone and which can be the simultaneous ends of everyone" (*LPed*, 9: 450). The child needs not an "*instructor*, who is merely a teacher," but a "*tutor*, who is a guide" (*LPed*, 9: 452), who must "prove" to the child that "restraint is put on it in order that it be led

---

18. Aquinas, *Summa Contra Gentiles*, III. 1, 37.1.

to the use of its own freedom, that it is cultivated so that it may one day be free" (*LPed*, 9: 454). It does not seem too much to suggest that Kant's *Groundwork* might be modeled on Kant's own conception of moral pedagogy, not giving "instructions," but "tutoring" us, which is to say, attempting to form us into cultivated, moralized, and thus free human beings.

In any case, if it is a problem for Kant's system that his fundamental principle must be interpreted to be applied, and that it is capable of more than one legitimate construal in similar situations, then this is also a problem for any other tradition of moral reasoning that aspires to the dizzy heights of a supreme principle that does not deliver prepackaged *a priori* answers to every moral dilemma and nuance. It is perhaps clearer on Kant's account what sort of action is wrong, rather than what sort of action is right. How would we know that a phenomenal action could not be a manifestation of a well-disposed noumenal self? We would know this, when it would be impossible to make a universal law out of the particular action being considered, in the sense that one could not ask everyone to assent to the principle I am promulgating. If I ask you to assent to a principle whereby everybody keeps their promises, except me when it suits my interests, I violate your project of end-setting (where you need to trust the promise in order to set an end), and so I go against the project of rational end-setting as such, and so against my own deep nature. Such a proposed course of action is at least blackballed as inconsistent with the project of universal and rational end-setting.

I have made a case for not objecting to the lack of detail that can seem to beset Kant's sheer moral position. Nonetheless, I would concede that perhaps Kant has an indecent amount of a good thing here. The virtue ethicist does not, at least, proclaim that the exercise of a moral disposition is fundamentally invisible. The utilitarian looks to manifest consequences, and the Thomist does think that free actions, turned toward the perfect freedom that is God, genuinely appear within nature, rather than lying beyond and behind the realm of that which appears. Nonetheless, I think that Kant's lack of specificity, and the need for application and interpretation, will not be the bedrock grounds upon which Kant's cousin, the Christian Platonist, will have the most anxiety about Kant. The bedrock disagreement will rather be this: Kant, because of his struggle to relate divine action and human freedom, has relocated God. God is no longer the all-satiating end of all our desires (and end-setting); rather, our highest good, replete with divinity, becomes identified with the sum total of all our mutual end-setting. In the next few pages, I explain this claim.

Christian Platonism and Christianized Platonism

I venture that the account of what Kant means by autonomy, set out above, would hardly seem obvious or intuitive to many contemporary people, even those who regard themselves as Kantian. There is a dizzying and vertiginous quality to it: our willing the end-setting as such, not because it is this particular end, or this person's end, but because it is an aspect of the plenitudinous project of all end-setting as such. In the effort to make some sort of sense of it, it can quickly be turned into something less mysterious: the value of seeking democratic consensus or justice; the value of self-expression; or the value of setting one's own goals. Some of these might be more amenable to Kant than others, although any effort to valorize an end because it is "mine" (the self-expression route), or because *I can set my own goal,* hardly looks promising. It is end-setting, the achievement of ends as such, that is valuable, not the fact that the end belongs to me, and certainly never because the ends express my empirically manifested and phenomenal desires. In truth, many so-called "Kantian" approaches Kant himself would consider to have unstable, empirical, and deleterious foundations, where moral foundations can only be safely found at the level of an adapted Platonism about perfectly rational human nature. This epistemically disciplined Platonism is perhaps better at ruling out premature solutions than at providing easy and generalizable answers. But in this, perhaps, it resembles something I celebrated about theology in the previous chapter, whereby a reference to transcendence can undercut hasty and totalizing ethical solutions that in the end dehumanize us.

I want to experiment with refraining, for a moment, from attempting to make sense of Kant's approach by projecting back upon him our own contemporary preoccupations about how to ground the content and motivation of morality. Here is an alternative suggestion. If we look at Kant's account of autonomy while holding in mind the categories of Christianized Platonic theology, mediated through rationalism, that we know Kant ascribes to, certain mysterious things take on a different aspect, and become limpid and transparent. The dizzying vertigo clears to reveal a landscape.

Casting our minds back to chapters two and three, what is it for God to create? God necessarily, but freely, as an expression of perfect freedom, wills to bring about the maximum possible degree of created reality and perfection. This arises as an expression of God's own nature, where God is the "all of reality." Only slightly tilting the vocabulary, we could talk of God realizing all of God's ends, where each "end" is the realization of an aspect of the divine being. The consequence of God's harmonious realization of all God's ends is divine blessedness, God's "well-pleasedness with himself which causes him to make these possibilities actual" (*LPR*, 28: 1061). God's act of creation is the realization of all real possibilities that are compatible with each other. This is something that all rational wills could universally will. We should be unsurprised then, when Kant tells us, at the height of his search for the supreme principle of morality, in the *Groundwork*, that God's "volition is of itself necessarily in accord with the law" (*GW*, 4: 414), such that "his maxims necessarily harmonize with the laws of *autonomy*" (*GW*, 4: 439, emphasis mine), because autonomy is the realization of all (really possible and co-possible) ends.

For the tradition represented by Thomas Aquinas, our highest created happiness is to participate in God's own happiness with Godself, in the happiness that is God. This is the "beatific vision." This is what will satiate all our desires, and be our joy forever. Dante has a foretaste of the beatific vision, of seeing "the high lamp which in Itself is true" (*Paradiso*, Canto XXXIII, line 54):

What then I saw is more than tongue can say.
Our human speech is dark before the vision.
The ravished memory swoons and falls away.
(*Paradiso*, Canto XXXIII, lines 55-57)

"On earth," Dante writes, "the mind is smoke," but in paradise, "it is fire" (*Paradiso*, XXI, line 100). Hoping only for a "single clue," as one "who sees in dreams" searches for "the emotional impression of his vision/ still powerful while its parts fade" (*Paradiso*, Canto XXXIII, lines 71, 58, 60), Dante recalls his glimpse of the being of God:

I saw within Its depth how It conceives
all things in a single volume bound by Love,
of which the universe is the scattered leaves.
(*Paradiso*, Canto XXXIII, lines 85-87)

Blessedness can only be achieved by knowing and contemplating God, which in turn can only be achieved by divine action upon us. This is the divine action that I spoke of in the previous chapter: an aspect of God's concurring action upon us, which is fully God's but fully our own, and which makes it possible for the dancer (us) to become the dance.

We know, though, that Kant could never accept this answer, because he rejects the possibility of "concursus." For Kant, our action must be our own, and not God's. If God were to act in us, it would cease to be our action. You simply cannot have a "beatific vision" if you share Kant's view about human freedom. At least, it makes it very difficult to say that the true perfection of the human creature lies in the contemplation of the perfection of God, and a participation in God's own happiness, which is happiness itself, the full and blazing source of all echoes and shadows of joy.

If there is to be perfection, and happiness subsequent upon perfection, it must, for Kant, be as a result of our own action, and not divine action. And this, I submit, is at the heart of the difference between Kant's religious conception of autonomy and the Christian Platonist tradition of thinking about happiness. Where in classical theology, happiness is found by participating in God's own self-knowledge, in Kant, we *achieve* happiness as a consequence of our willing, according to the project of rational end-setting. The project of end-setting does not find its resting place in God's beatific vision, where all desires are satiated, but is done by us, as noumenal willers projecting out and receiving each other's ends. We are in a community of equals, of other noumenal willers and end-setters. Kant tells us that happiness is not our goal, but that it would be the consequence of everyone in fact realizing autonomy, that is, of everyone engaging in the project of rational end-setting, where we have "the hope of some day participating in happiness to the degree that we have been intent upon not being unworthy of it" (*CPrR*, 5: 130).

What is Kant's equivalent, on this picture, of the "beatific vision"? It is simply this: to be in a community of rational end-setters, mutually endorsing the project of end-setting as such, and not because it is this particular end, or my end, or the end of this particular person. There is a relationship to traditional Platonism, in that there is a drive to a sort of fullness of perfection, and plenitude of reality, a satiation of as much (noumenal) desire and end-setting as is possible. But there is a willing community, rather than a participatory hierarchy.

In the second *Critique*, as we saw in chapter three, Kant insists that we must believe in God in order to guarantee the achievement of the highest good, of which happiness is a part, that ought to arise from our autonomous willing in rational community. But, really, when we consider Kant's denial of the possibility of human-divine concursus, what *really* can God do for us? How could God guarantee happiness? It really is up to us. God, Kant tells us, is indeed to be found in the noumenal "kingdom of ends," but more as a first among equals than as the plenitudinous source of all reality. God cannot make us happy. Our happiness consists in our willing autonomously. For some reason, we do not do so. We turn away from the project of rational end-setting as such, stretching out instead toward partial, selfish, and therefore irrational ends, which destroy the project of rational and universal end-setting. But if we ever did stop turning away from autonomy, it would be by our own striving, and not because of divine action.

In chapter three, I said that, for Kant, only a God could save us. Now it looks, though, as if not even a God can save us. We must save ourselves. We must be our own divinity, or rather, reason in us is our divinity, if divinity is the source of happiness and salvation. And this is why Kant's strange final theosis in the *Opus Postumum* is an insightful unveiling of a deep truth that has always resided in Kant's theology: that, ultimately, God cannot save or transform us, if God is alien to our freedom and our own rational end-setting. Our main hope must be in ourselves, and in our reason. As early as the 1770s, Kant seems to come close to this insight in a *Reflexion,* where he writes:

> The moral feeling can only be set into motion by the image of a world full of order, if we place ourselves in this world in thought. This is the intellectual world, whose bond is God. We are in part really in this world, insofar as human beings really judge in accordance with moral principles. (Happiness would be the **natural** consequence of that, which is something entirely different from the merely arbitrary happiness through divine providence, in that we would create our good fortune for ourselves and could really bring it to such a moral world-order.) (*R* 1171, 1772-75, 15: 518)

Kant expresses a similar thought in 1781, in the first *Critique,* writing that "in the moral world," "the realization of which rests on the [for us always unrealized] condition that **everyone** do what he should," "a system of happiness proportionately combined with morality can also be thought as necessary":

> Since freedom . . . would itself be the cause of the general happiness, and rational beings, under the guidance of such principles, would themselves be the authors of their own enduring welfare and at the same time that of others. (A 809-10/B 837-38)

It is not that God, in such a picture, does "nothing." God plays some sort of role, but only the minimal one of ensuring that the "moral world," wherein we find the highest good, operates according to a "rule" that guarantees "appropriate consequences" (A 811/B 839), such that "happiness" is distributed "in exact proportion with the morality of rational beings" (A 814/B 842). God becomes the name for a principle of stability, a principle of divinity, whereby morality leads to happiness. This is in contrast to the traditional picture, where God is a willing and acting being, acting even within our freedom. God, for Kant, does not act within us to make us moral, and God is not the transforming object or end of our striving and desiring.

It was never very clear what the other religious postulate of "immortality" did for Kant, other than being a mythological evocation of our true status as not being temporal at all. As we saw in chapter three, Kant writes in 1793 about the "*highest good*" coming about "through our cooperation" (*TP*, 8: 280n). This is at least suggestive of a line of thought in the *Opus Postumum*. Where formerly Kant insisted that one had to postulate the existence of God to secure the highest good, Kant now intimates that we must postulate progress in history, as a phenomenal manifestation, the moving image of eternity, of our own noumenal turning toward autonomy. And that would indeed be where we would need to find our hope: not in God, but in ourselves, as divine.

Running throughout Kant's practical philosophy is an explicit aversion to all "external objects." The language of "external objects" reaches back to the medieval terminology of an "object" *(obiectus)* of the understanding or will. So, for Aquinas, the will must always have an "object" toward which it is inclined. The only ultimately satiating "object" is the truth itself in all plenitude, which is God. To say, according to this usage, that God is the object of the understanding or will is in no way to imply that God is "an object," any more than we imply that "the essence of poetry" is an object, if we make the object of our thought the essence of poetry. The extent of Kant's aversion to *all* and *any* external object can be overlooked by commentators, who tend to emphasize the more obviously inadequate candidates for being a worthy object of our attention or desire. For example, it is clear that an arbitrary command could never, for Kant, be a worthy object for us. Nor could a fleeting sensation or impulse be a worthy object. Nothing with a contingent duration in time and extension in space could be such a worthy object. But Kant is clear not only that he rejects unworthy external objects to the will, but *all* external objects, in the capacious sense of the Latin *obiectus* — that which is presented to the understanding or will.

Kant insists that "if the will" seeks the law "in a property of any of its objects — *heteronomy* always results":

> The will in that case does not give itself the law; instead the object *(das Object),* by means of its relation to the will, gives the law to it. (*GW* II, 4: 441)

Kant is clear that this is the case, whether the influence of the external object is exerted by sensuous "inclination" or by "representations of reason" (*GW* II, 4: 441). Kant regards as heteronomous *all* the "objects" of the will and intellect surveyed by the previous tradition, sensible and rational, created and uncreated. That Kant is convinced of the unsuitability of all external objects, created and uncreated, is made clear in Section II of the *Groundwork:*

> Wherever an object of the will has to be laid down as the basis for prescribing the rule that determines the will, there the rule is none other than heteronomy; the imperative is conditional, namely: *if* or *because* one wills this object, one ought to act in such and such a way: hence it can never command morally, that is, categorically. (*GW* II, 4: 444)

This is the case, Kant explains, whether "the object determines the will by means of inclination" or by means of "reason directed to objects of our possible volition in general" (*GW* II, 4: 444). Among external objects Kant includes the "the principle of perfection" (*GW* II, 4: 444; see also *GW* II, 4: 410). Even if the will was moved by representations of reason pertaining to a principle of perfection, this would still involve the will being moved by an "incentive," such that freedom is impossible. Consider the list of potential external objects that Kant rejects in the *Groundwork.* It includes "human nature," "perfection," "happiness," "moral feeling," and "fear of God" (*GW* II, 4: 410). Kant insists he desires a "completely isolated metaphysics of morals":

> Mixed with no anthropology, theology, physics, or hyperphysics and still less with occult qualities (which could be called hypophysical). (*GW* II, 4:410)

Even the concepts of "ontological perfection" and "theological perfection" are ruled out of consideration (*GW* II, 4: 443), by which Kant rules out the concept of the perfection of the divine nature, and the divine will. If we are acted upon by any external object, no matter how elevated, created or uncreated, we would "at bottom" enjoy "nothing better than the freedom of a turnspit" (*CPrR*, 5: 97).

This is a stark, strong, and innovative demand upon autonomy.[19] If we really can have no external object, no matter how elevated, created or uncreated, then some recent so-called "value realist" readings of Kant are called into question.[20] These readings suggest that Kant does in fact have fairly traditional and substantial commitments to a notion of human flourishing or moral goodness, and that he understands these to be compatible with autonomy. "Heteronomy" only threatens when the external object is something arbitrary, capricious, or unstable (such as an impulse, or an arbitrary command). If we were to contemplate the shape of the good for our rational nature, or the perfection of God, then there could be no danger to autonomy, so long as we are able, by our own lights, to recognize and acknowledge the perfection that we follow. Attractive as these reconstructions are, Kant just does hold out a deeper and stranger objection against any external object *(Object/obiectus)* at all, even the uncreated good that is God, or the perfection of rational nature.

Kant knows that an external object need not be desire or pleasure, but can be the shape of perfection for rational nature, or the plenitude that is the uncreated God. But always the problem is *freedom*. If we are moved toward, or by, an external object, we are not free, even if it is God moving

19. The distinctive nature of this dramatic innovation, rejecting any external object, however elevated, created or uncreated, is neglected in accounts that stress lines of continuity between Kant's concept of autonomy and earlier intellectualist approaches to ethics. See, for example, Terence Irwin, "Continuity in the History of Autonomy," *Inquiry: An Interdisciplinary Journal of Philosophy* 54.5 (2011): 442-59; Stephen Darwall, *The British Moralists and the Internal "Ought": 1640-1740* (Cambridge: Cambridge University Press, 1995); and J. B. Schneewind, *The Invention of Autonomy: A History of Modern Moral Philosophy* (Cambridge: Cambridge University Press, 2005).

20. See, for example, Robert Stern, *Understanding Moral Obligation: Kant, Hegel, Kierkegaard* (Cambridge: Cambridge University Press, 2012), chap. 1; Allen W. Wood, *Kant's Ethical Thought* (Cambridge: Cambridge University Press, 1999); Irwin, "Continuity"; and Irwin's *The Development of Ethics: A Historical and Critical Study*, vol. 3: *From Kant to Rawls* (Oxford: Oxford University Press, 2009), pp. 163-68. Irwin, for example, claims that Kant is only hostile to "incentives that are not essential to a rational will" (p. 164), but not "to an objective reality that guides the will" (p. 164). As I show above, this is wrong. Kant precisely does object to any sort of external reality. For a more extensive consideration of these issues, see my "A Thomistic Reading of Kant's *Groundwork of the Metaphysics of Morals:* Searching for the Unconditioned," *Modern Theology* 31.2 (2015): 284-311.

within us. This is what is involved in the rejection of concurrence accounts of divine action and human freedom. It is a far more significant rupture with the Christian tradition than any supposed crisis in belief in the existence of God. Kant believes in God. It is our freedom in relation to such a God that he cannot believe in, at least in a traditional sense. If we are to be free, the will must have no external efficient cause, and no external object.

Kant insists that inasmuch as we are free, the will's object must in fact come subsequent to the will's action. It must come downstream of the will. For Aquinas, the key to our nature is that we have received all that we have from elsewhere, *ab alio,* and that we are thus shot through in all that we are and do by heteronomy.[21] Heteronomy is our wound, where our wound is our essence and our only hope. Heteronomy, for Kant, is an assault on our proper dignity as human. In the end, then, Kant must be said to reject a key strand of Christian theology. He rejects the claim that the ultimate object of theology (God) can be a worthy object for us.

By a circuitous route, I am in agreement with some secular construals of Kant's moral philosophy, which understand that the moral law must be the product, not the object, of our rational end-setting.[22] But the agreement is limited to the conclusion, and not to the way in which Kant gets there. Kant's journey to this conclusion, as traced in this book, remains saturated in metaphysical and theological commitments, and is itself the product of these commitments, rather than being an alternative to them. Kant's mature and final movements of thought still have a theological shape. This is because Kant is concerned with what would be a worthy object for a rational being, whose dignity is such that the object of attention must not be in any sense external. This is the oldest theological problem of all, reaching back through Aquinas, and back to Aristotle and Plato, gravitating toward a version of the perennial answer, "thought thinking itself."

The particular harmonic that Kant sounds on this great melody is that the "object" of the rational will must be the will's own giving to itself of that which it can rationally will for itself, the universal law. Autonomy contains within it the echo of an ancient perennial theology, perhaps more Platonic than Christian, in that the Platonic exhortation is always to "become God" through self-transcending pure reason, rather than by waiting upon a gra-

21. I am indebted here to Josef Pieper, *Happiness and Contemplation* (New York: Pantheon, 1958), pp. 22ff.

22. See, for example, Korsgaard, *Creating the Kingdom of Ends*; also her *The Sources of Normativity* (Cambridge: Cambridge University Press, 1996).

cious God who condescends, saves, and transforms. This ancient Platonic aspiration can be detected in the fragmentary final writings of Kant, discussed above, where Kant denies that God is a "*substance* outside myself, whose existence I postulate as a hypothetical being" (*OP,* 22: 123). Rather, "I, man, am this being myself" (*OP,* 21: 25). Our moral commanding itself has the mark of divinity: "the spirit of man, under a compulsion which is only possible through *freedom*" (*OP,* 21: 25). From this divine activity, Kant writes, "emerges" "a God" thought "in human practical reason." While "all expressions of moral-practical reason are divine," in that they "contain the moral imperative," "it is not God in substance whose existence is proved" (*OP,* 21: 26). "The commanding subject," Kant writes, "is God," where "this commanding being is not outside man as a substance different from man" (*OP,* 21: 22):

> "There is a God," namely, in human, moral-practical reason . . . "we are originally of divine race" with regard to our vocation and its dispositions. (*OP,* 21: 30)

The only worthy object for the rational will is ourselves, but not ourselves as we are, but ourselves as we become pure reason, and so become divine. A striking and perennial feature of secular Kantian approaches is an appeal to a sort of "God's eye point of view," or "original position," that human beings ought to aspire to, at least in our conceptual imagination. Such a perspective is nicely evocative of the way in which human reason comes to take on aspects of "divinity" for the late Kant of the *Opus Postumum.*

A number of times throughout this book I have talked of Kant as having a "theology," a "spirituality" even. At the same time, I have also expressed doubts about the appropriateness of calling Kant a "Christian." At the heart of this has been Kant's struggle to relate divine action and human freedom. We have seen this difficulty cascade into every area of doctrine, including incarnation, trinity, atonement, and grace. Kant, in the end, is unable to say very much about divine action and revelation, and is unable to embrace elements of faith that the tradition regards as mysteries, which transcend reason while also satisfying it. Given that Kant is not (straightforwardly) a "Christian," in what sense can a Christian theologian call Kant's system of thought a type of "theology"?[23]

In fact, there is a very precise sense in which the Christian tradition

---

23. I am grateful to Nathaniel Warne, for pushing me to engage with this question.

can call Kant's philosophy about God "theology." In the opening question of the *Summa Theologiae*, Aquinas reflects that "the philosophical sciences deal with all parts of reality, even with God," so that "Aristotle refers to one department of philosophy as theology or the divine science" (*ST*, I, 1). When thinking about God, Aquinas writes:

> There is nothing to stop the same things being treated by the philosophical sciences when they can be looked at in the light of natural reason and by another science when they are looked at in the light of divine revelation. (*ST*, I, 1)

As we have already seen in chapters three and five, Kant explicitly associates himself with an ambitious and classical understanding of philosophy. Philosophy, on this conception, involves a search for wisdom. This search brings about a participation in, and identification with, self-transcending, harmonious, and universal reason. Reason, so conceived, is a type of divinity, such that when we pattern ourselves according to it, we become divine. In that revelation and mystery are not essential components of "reason as divinity," such a conception of philosophy is covered by Aquinas's description of "philosophy as theology," which reflects upon "all parts of reality," even up to "God," without recourse to revelation or holy teaching.

Reading Kant as a devotee of "classical philosophy" provides illumination on a number of fronts. First of all, it invites us to expand our categories when engaging with Kant, and also with a range of Enlightenment philosophers and writers at the origins of modernity. At present, commentators tend to gravitate toward one of three interpretative options when reading figures such as Kant, or other expansive and systematic Enlightenment thinkers such as Descartes and Leibniz. One option is to read these thinkers in a naturalistic and secular way, reading out of them, as much as possible, theological and "extravagant" metaphysical commitments. A second option is to maximize Christian elements and orthodoxy. A third option is to treat such philosophers as deviant Christians, falling away from the tradition into various forms of heterodoxy, heresy, and error. But perhaps we get closer to the heart of this strand of modernity by adopting a fourth way, which is to read Kant, and others, as faithful custodians of a more cosmological and visionary conception of philosophy, which is not naturalist, secular, Christian, or heretical. We are used to the idea that "theology" is squeezed out of our interpretations of "modernity." This has been so often

153

said and lamented, though, that it can hardly anymore be the case. Perhaps the tradition that is genuinely occluded and forgotten is the "Philosophy" in philosophy ("philosophical philosophy"), which affirms and believes in God and divinity, but which, on principled grounds, engages only with what reason (albeit expansively understood) can show, rather than with revelation and mystery.

What attitude, then, might the Christian theologian have to "philosophy" so conceived, "theology as philosophy"? A theologian informed by Thomas Aquinas will have, I suspect, a range of reactions that are complex, but not confused or complicated.[24] First of all, Aquinas is clear that "philosophy as theology" differs "in kind" from the "theology of holy teaching," that is, from Christian theology, which begins and ends in the divine self-revelation given in Scripture. Christian theology, sacred doctrine, will incorporate and use philosophical tools, but only to explicate, apply, and defend the mysteries and articles of faith. We are led here to one of the great perennial distinctions between "philosophy as theology" and "theology as sacred doctrine." Theology begins and ends in revelation and divine action. "Philosophy as theology" will not give such precedence or status to revelation and mystery, but ask rather what "natural reason" can achieve, with the vital qualification that the categories of both nature and reason are conceived of in vastly richer terms than we have now become accustomed to.

In one obvious sense, of course, the Thomist theologian will not endorse, or practice, "theology as philosophy," as articulated by Kant. Certainly, the Thomist will insist that *this* is not Christian theology, as practiced in the tradition. But the more subtle and generous Thomist will not straightforwardly "condemn" philosophy as theology, any more than Thomas does. When "theology as philosophy" is practiced with discipline and self-reflection, there is even a type of implicit, if unintended, *homage* to theology as revelation. Kant's intellectual endeavor over the arc of a whole lifetime is a type of *askesis* of reason, asking always and only about the limits and boundaries of "mere" reason. By marking these out with such discipline and reserve, Kant, in a way, is more theologically faithful and respectful than other philosophers, who reach more greedily into the realm of doctrine. Even where Kant does discuss religious doctrine, he does so, explicitly and studiedly, within the self-set boundaries of "mere reason." There is, in Kant, a principled refusal to speak, an

24. In shaping my thinking here, I am indebted to conversation with Ben DeSpain.

apophatic quiet, where philosophy, even on a visionary conception, may not go. In "seeing as reason sees," Kant sets the limits of reason. As Dante might both approve of and regret Virgil's reticence and withdrawal, the theologian might both approve of and regret Kant's retreat from mystery and revelation.

An observation made by John Henry Newman is relevant here. Newman comments that "it is not the profound thinkers who intrude with their discussions and criticisms within the sacred limits" of theology:

> A really philosophical mind, if unhappily it has ruined its own religious perceptions, will be silent; it will understand that Religion does not lie in its way: it may disbelieve its truths, it may account belief in them a weakness, or, on the other hand, a happy dream, a delightful error, which it cannot itself enjoy; — any how, it will not usurp.[25]

Reciprocally, perhaps, the "philosopher," on the more classical conception, could regard with complex approval, and regret, the theologian who embraces revelation and mystery: approval, inasmuch as the theologian is led to philosophical truth, and regret, perhaps, at the means of doing so. More subtly, there might also be, as there is in Kant, a self-studied and apophatic refusal to have a *philosophical* position on that which goes beyond, or falls below, what philosophy can say. As we have seen, Kant rejects the notion that certain doctrines or theological commitments, such as concursus, have any application in either theoretical or practical reason. Nonetheless, Kant is still capable of the nuanced reflection that although concursus is "inconceivable," and not to be philosophically employed by us, nonetheless "our reason cannot deny the possibility of this *concursus*" (*LPR*, 28: 1106). In this space, of what reason by itself can neither use nor deny, theology will do much of its work. It would be too strong a statement to say that Kant practices apophatic theology, if, by this, we mean that he reflects upon the role of silence, mystery, and unknowing in the life of faith. It seems less inappropriate to say that Kant is apophatic about theology, given the limitations of what reason can see and say.

---

25. John Henry Newman, "The Usurpations of Reason," in John Henry Newman, *Fifteen Sermons Preached Before the University of Oxford Between A.D. 1826 and 1843* (Notre Dame: University of Notre Dame Press, 2003), Sermon IV.16, p. 68.

Conclusion

So we return to Kant's graveside as the coffin is lowered in the earth. Are we still certain that Scheffner is correct to tremble as Kant's mortal remains are lowered? In a sense, Kant has achieved in his dying reflections what he never could in his mature critical philosophy. In the previous chapter, I meditated on W. B. Yeats's question:

> O body swayed to music, O brightening glance,
> How can we know the dancer from the dance?
> (W. B. Yeats, "Among School Children")

In becoming our own divinity, Kant manages finally to identify the dancer and the dance. Some of the sad anecdotes from Kant's last days — electric cats, poisonous beer, and cheese addiction — need to be counterbalanced by other stories.

Three years before his death, Kant explained to his friends:

> My gentlemen, I am not afraid of death; I will know how to die. I assure you before God [perhaps, now Kant means, the divinity within all humanity] that, should I feel in the coming night that [I should die] I would fold my hands and say "God be praised."[26]

It "would be different," Kant went on to say, if he was to be told on his deathbed, "You have made human beings unhappy."[27] On his deathbed, Kant woke from his slumber to tell his surprised doctor, "the feeling of humanity has not yet left me": and we know what the concept of "humanity" now represents for Kant, approaching as it does divinity.[28] Kant's last words were the enigmatic "*es ist gut,*" "it is good." We cannot know the scope of this claim: death, life, the universe, or the bread and wine that he had just been given by his friend Wasianski. In any case Jachmann describes the moment of death. Kant "died as calmly as is possible, without any distortions and without any sign of a violent separation, but seemingly gladly."[29]

26. Kuehn, *Biography,* p. 414.
27. Kuehn, *Biography,* p. 414.
28. Kuehn, *Biography,* p. 422.
29. Kuehn, *Biography,* p. 422.

Further Reading

Chapter Two

Kant biography:

Kuehn, Manfred. *Kant: A Biography.* Cambridge: Cambridge University Press, 2001.
Wood, Allen W. "Kant's Life and Works." In *A Companion to Kant.* Edited by Graham Bird. Oxford: Wiley-Blackwell, 2010. Pp. 10-31.

On Kant's rationalist theology:

Insole, Christopher J. *Kant and the Creation of Freedom: A Theological Problem.* Oxford: Oxford University Press, 2013. Chapters 2-3.
Wood, Allen W. *Kant's Rational Theology.* Ithaca, NY: Cornell University Press, 1970.

On Kant's proof of the existence of God from possibility:

Chignell, Andrew. "Kant, Modality and the Most Real Being." *Archiv für Geschichte der Philosophie* 91.2 (2009): 157-92.
Stang, Nicholas. "Kant's Possibility Proof." *History of Philosophy Quarterly* 27.3 (2010): 275-99.

On the debate around "real possibility" and essences:

Bird, Alexander. "Necessarily Salt Dissolves in Water." *Analysis* 61 (2001): 267-74.
Ellis, Brian. *Scientific Essentialism.* Cambridge: Cambridge University Press, 2001.
Insole, Christopher J. "Intellectualism, Relational Properties and the Divine Mind in Kant's Pre-Critical Philosophy." *Kantian Review* 16.3 (2011): 399-428.

———. *Kant and the Creation of Freedom.* Oxford: Oxford University Press, 2013. Chapter 3.

Langton, Rae. *Kantian Humility: Our Ignorance of Things in Themselves.* Oxford: Oxford University Press, 2004. Chapter 5.

Mumford, Stephen. *Laws in Nature.* London: Routledge, 2004.

Chapter Three

Theologically informed accounts of the development of Kant's thought from the pre-critical into the critical period:

Insole, Christopher J. *Kant and the Creation of Freedom: A Theological Problem.* Oxford: Oxford University Press, 2013.

Laywine, Alison. *Kant's Early Metaphysics and the Origins of the Critical Philosophy.* Atascadero, CA: Ridgeview, 1993.

Ward, Keith. *The Development of Kant's View of Ethics.* Oxford: Blackwell, 1972.

Wood, Allen W. *Kant's Rational Theology.* Ithaca, NY: Cornell University Press, 1970.

On the interpretation of the concept of the highest good:

Auxter, Thomas. "The Unimportance of the Highest Good." *History of Philosophy Quarterly* 17 (1979): 121-34.

Beiser, Frederick. "Moral Faith and the Highest Good." In *The Cambridge Companion to Kant and Modern Philosophy.* Edited by Paul Guyer. Cambridge: Cambridge University Press, 2002. Pp. 588-629.

Friedman, R. Z. "The Importance and Function of Kant's Highest Good." *Journal of the History of Philosophy* 22 (1984): 325-42.

Insole, Christopher. "The Irreducible Importance of Religious Hope in Kant's Conception of the Highest Good." *Philosophy* 83.3 (2008): 333-51.

———. "Kant on Christianity, Religion and Politics: Three Hopes, Three Limits." *Studies in Christian Ethics,* forthcoming (2016).

Marina, Jacqueline. "Making Sense of Kant's Highest Good." *Kant-Studien* 91 (2000): 329-55.

Pasternack, Lawrence. "The Development and Scope of Kantian Belief: The Highest Good, the Practical Postulates and the Fact of Reason." *Kant-Studien* 102 (2011): 290-315.

———. *Routledge Philosophy Guidebook to Kant on Religion within the Boundaries of Mere Reason.* London and New York: Routledge, 2014. Chapter 1.

Reath, Andrews. "Two Conceptions of the Highest Good in Kant." *Journal of the History of Philosophy* 26.4 (1988): 593-619.

Silber, John. "The Importance of the Highest Good in Kant's Ethics." *Ethics* 73 (1963): 179-95.

———. "Kant's Conception of the Highest Good as Immanent and Transcendent." *Philosophical Review* 68 (1959): 460-92.

Simmons, Lance. "Kant's Highest Good: Albatross, Keystone, Achilles' Heel." *History of Philosophy Quarterly* 10.4 (1993): 355-68.

On interpretations of Kant as a divine command theorist:

Hare, John. *God and Morality: A Philosophical History.* Oxford: Wiley-Blackwell, 2009. Pp. 122-75.

———. *God's Call: Moral Realism, God's Commands, and Human Autonomy.* Grand Rapids: Eerdmans, 2001. Pp. 87-119.

———. "Kant on Recognizing our Duties as God's Commands." *Faith and Philosophy* 17 (2000): 459-78.

———. "Kant's Divine Command Theory and Its Reception within Analytical Philosophy." In *Kant and Kierkegaard on Religion.* Edited by D. Z. Phillips and Timothy Tessin. New York: Palgrave Macmillan, 2000. Pp. 263-77.

Stern, Robert. *Understanding Moral Obligation: Kant, Hegel, Kierkegaard.* Cambridge: Cambridge University Press, 2012. Pp. 75-88.

On the role of practical reason in forming warranted belief, and different textures of assent:

Chignell, Andrew. "Belief in Kant." *Philosophical Review* 116.3 (2007): 323-60.

———. "Kant's Concepts of Justification." *Noûs* 41.1 (2007): 33-63.

Ferreira, M. Jamie. "Hope, Virtue, and the Postulate of God: A Reappraisal of Kant's Pure Practical Rational Belief." *Religious Studies* 50 (2014): 3-26.

Gardner, Sebastian. "The Primacy of Practical Reason." In *A Companion to Kant.* Edited by Graham Bird. Oxford: Wiley-Blackwell, 2010. Pp. 259-74.

Insole, Christopher J. *Kant and the Creation of Freedom: A Theological Problem.* Oxford: Oxford University Press, 2013. Chapter 7.

Pasternack, Lawrence. "The Development and Scope of Kantian Belief: The Highest Good, the Practical Postulates, and the Fact of Reason." *Kant-Studien* 102 (2011): 290-315.

———. "Kant on Opinion: Assent, Hypothesis, and the Norms of General Applied Logic." *Kant-Studien* 105.1 (2014): 41-82.

———. "Regulative Principles and 'the Wise Author of Nature.'" *Religious Studies* 47.4 (2011): 411-29.

Stevenson, Leslie. "Opinion, Belief or Faith, and Knowledge." *Kantian Review* 7 (2003): 72-101.

Deflationary accounts of Kant's critical philosophy of religion:

Byrne, Peter. *Kant on God.* Aldershot: Ashgate, 2007.
Guyer, Paul. *Kant.* London: Routledge, 2006. Chapters 3 and 6.

Sympathetic accounts of Kant's critical philosophy of religion:

Anderson, Pamela Sue, and Jordan Bell. *Kant and Theology.* London and New
 York: T&T Clark International, 2010.
DiCenso, James. *Kant's Religion within the Boundaries of Mere Reason.* Cambridge:
 Cambridge University Press, 2012.
Firestone, Chris L. *Kant and Theology at the Boundaries of Reason.* Aldershot:
 Ashgate, 2009.
Firestone, Chris L., and Nathan Jacobs. *In Defense of Kant's Religion.* Bloomington:
 Indiana University Press, 2008.
Moore, Adrian. *Noble in Reason, Infinite in Faculty: Themes and Variations in Kant's
 Moral and Religious Philosophy.* London: Routledge, 2003.
Palmquist, Stephen. *Kant's Critical Religion,* vol. 2 of *Kant's System of Perspectives.*
 Aldershot: Ashgate, 2000.
Wood, Allen W. *Kant's Moral Religion.* Ithaca, NY: Cornell University Press, 1970.
———. *Kant's Rational Theology.* Ithaca, NY: Cornell University Press, 1970.

Discussions of Kant's moral proof for the existence of God:

Hare, John. *The Moral Gap: Kantian Ethics, Human Limits, and God's Assistance.*
 Oxford: Clarendon Press, 1996.
Insole, Christopher J. "The Irreducible Importance of Religious Hope in Kant's
 Conception of the Highest Good." *Philosophy* 83.3 (2008): 333-51.
Wood, Allen W. *Kant's Moral Religion.* Ithaca, NY: Cornell University Press, 1970.

Chapter Four

On the pre-critical Kant's views about causation and freedom:

Byrd, Jeremy. "Kant's Compatibilism in the New Elucidation of the First Principles
 of Metaphysical Cognition." *Kant-Studien* 99.1 (2008): 68-79.
Friedman, Michael. *Kant and the Exact Sciences.* Cambridge, MA: Harvard Uni-
 versity Press, 1992.
Laywine, Alison. *Kant's Early Metaphysics and the Origins of the Critical Philosophy.*
 Atascadero, CA: Ridgeview, 1993.
Watkins, Eric. *Kant and the Metaphysics of Causality.* Cambridge: Cambridge Uni-
 versity Press, 2005.

Further Reading

On the influence of Rousseau on Kant:

Cassirer, Ernst. *Rousseau-Kant-Goethe: Two Essays.* Princeton: Princeton University Press, 1947.

Velkley, Richard L. *Freedom and the End of Reason: On the Moral Foundation of Kant's Critical Philosophy.* Chicago: University of Chicago Press, 1989.

On Kant's shift toward a non-compatibilist conception of freedom:

Hogan, Desmond. "Three Kinds of Rationalism and the Non-Spatiality of Things in Themselves." *Journal of the History of Philosophy* 47.3 (2009): 355-82.

Insole, Christopher J. *Kant and the Creation of Freedom: A Theological Problem.* Oxford: Oxford University Press, 2013. Chapter 4.

Chapter Five

On Swedenborg's influence on Kant and "Dreams of a Spirit-Seer":

Laywine, Alison. *Kant's Early Metaphysics and the Origins of the Critical Philosophy.* Atascadero, CA: Ridgeview, 1993.

Palmquist, Stephen. *Kant's Critical Religion,* vol. 2 of *Kant's System of Perspectives.* Aldershot: Ashgate, 2000.

Ward, Keith. *The Development of Kant's View of Ethics.* Oxford: Blackwell, 1972. Chapter 3.

On the relationship between freedom and Kant's solution to his crisis about knowledge:

Ameriks, Karl. *Interpreting Kant's Critiques.* Oxford: Oxford University Press, 2003. Chapter 6.

Hogan, Desmond. "How to Know Unknowable Things in Themselves." *Noûs* 43.1 (2009): 49-63.

———. "Kant's Copernican Turn and the Rationalist Tradition." In *The Cambridge Companion to Kant's Critique of Pure Reason.* Edited by Paul Guyer. Cambridge: Cambridge University Press, 2010. Pp. 21-40.

———. "Noumenal Affection." *Philosophical Review* 118.4 (2009): 501-32.

———. "Three Kinds of Rationalism and the Non-Spatiality of Things in Themselves." *Journal of the History of Philosophy* 47.3 (2009): 355-82.

On the relationship between God, human freedom, and Kant's solution to his crisis about knowledge:

Insole, Christopher J. *Kant and the Creation of Freedom: A Theological Problem.* Oxford: Oxford University Press, 2013.

————. "Kant's Transcendental Idealism and Newton's Divine Sensorium." *Journal of the History of Ideas* 72.3 (2011): 413-36.

————. "Kant's Transcendental Idealism, Freedom, and the Divine Mind." *Modern Theology* 27.4 (2011): 608-38.

Chapter Six

On the interpretation of transcendental idealism:

Allison, Henry. "Kant's Transcendental Idealism." In *A Companion to Kant.* Edited by Graham Bird. Oxford: Wiley-Blackwell, 2010. Pp. 111-24.

Ameriks, Karl. *Interpreting Kant's Critiques.* Oxford: Oxford University Press, 2003.

Bennett, Jonathan. *Kant's Analytic.* Cambridge: Cambridge University Press, 1966.

————. *Kant's Dialectic.* Cambridge: Cambridge University Press, 1974.

Chignell, Andrew. "Real Repugnance and Belief about Things-in-Themselves: A Problem and Kant's Three Solutions." In *Kant's Moral Metaphysics: God, Freedom and Immortality.* Edited by Benjamin Lipscomb and James Kreuger. New York: De Gruyter, 2010. Pp. 177-209.

————. "Real Repugnance and Our Ignorance of Things-in-Themselves: A Lockean Problem in Kant and Hegel." In *Internationales Jahrbuch des Deutschen Idealismus* 7. Edited by F. Rush, K. Ameriks, and J. Stolzenberg. Berlin: Walter de Gruyter, 2010.

Hogan, Desmond. "Kant's Copernican Turn and the Rationalist Tradition." In *The Cambridge Companion to Kant's Critique of Pure Reason.* Edited by Paul Guyer. Cambridge: Cambridge University Press, 2010. Pp. 21-40.

————. "Noumenal Affection." *Philosophical Review* 118.4 (2009): 501-32.

Insole, Christopher J. "Kant and the Creation of Freedom: A Response to Terry Godlove." *International Journal for the Philosophy of Religion* 77 (2014): 111-28.

————. *Kant and the Creation of Freedom: A Theological Problem.* Oxford: Oxford University Press, 2013. Chapter 5.

Merrihew Adams, Robert. "Things in Themselves." *Philosophy and Phenomenological Research* 57.4 (1997): 801-25.

Strawson, Peter. *The Bounds of Sense: An Essay on Kant's Critique of Pure Reason.* London: Methuen, 1966.

On the incoherence of transcendental freedom/noumenal causation:

Insole, Christopher J. *Kant and the Creation of Freedom: A Theological Problem.* Oxford: Oxford University Press, 2013. Chapter 6.

Pereboom, Derk. "Kant on Transcendental Freedom." *Philosophy and Phenomenological Research* 73.3 (2006): 537-64.

Walker, Ralph. *Kant.* London: Routledge and Kegan Paul, 1978.

On Kant and the inability to explain evil actions:

Duncan, Samuel. "Moral Evil, Freedom and the Goodness of God: Why Kant Abandoned Theodicy." *British Journal for the History of Philosophy* 20.5 (2012): 973-91.

Insole, Christopher J. *Kant and the Creation of Freedom: A Theological Problem.* Oxford: Oxford University Press, 2013. Chapter 6.

Kilby, Karen. "Evil and the Limits of Theology." *New Blackfriars* 84.983 (2003): 13-29.

Michalson, Gordon. *Fallen Freedom: Kant on Radical Evil and Moral Regeneration.* Cambridge: Cambridge University Press, 1990.

Chapter Seven

On concurrence accounts of divine and creaturely action:

Burrell, David. "Divine Action and Human Freedom in the Context of Creation." In *The God Who Acts: Philosophical and Theological Explorations.* University Park: Penn State University Press, 1994. Pp. 103-9.

———. *Freedom and Creation in Three Traditions.* Notre Dame: University of Notre Dame Press, 1993.

Freddoso, Alfred J. "God's General Concurrence with Secondary Causes: Pitfalls and Prospects." *American Catholic Philosophical Quarterly* 67 (1994): 131-56.

———. "God's General Concurrence with Secondary Causes: Why Conservation Is Not Enough." *Philosophical Perspectives* 5 (1991): 553-85.

———. "Medieval Aristotelianism and the Case against Secondary Causation in Nature." In *Divine and Human Action: Essays in the Metaphysics of Theism.* Edited by Thomas V. Morris. Ithaca: Cornell University Press, 1988. Pp. 74-118.

Tanner, Kathryn. *God and Creation in Christian Theology: Tyranny or Empowerment?* Minneapolis: Fortress Press, 2005.

———. "Human Freedom, Human Sin, and God the Creator." In *The God Who*

Acts: Philosophical and Theological Explorations. Edited by Thomas F. Tracy. University Park: Penn State University Press, 1994. Pp. 111-36.

Critiques of concurrence accounts:

Flint, Thomas. "Two Accounts of Providence." In *Divine and Human Action: Essays in the Metaphysics of Theism.* Edited by Thomas V. Morris. Ithaca, NY: Cornell University Press, 1988.

Hasker, William. "God the Creator of Good and Evil?" In *The God Who Acts: Philosophical and Theological Explorations.* Edited by Thomas F. Tracy. University Park: Penn State University Press, 1994. Pp. 137-46.

On Kant's critique of concurrence:

Insole, Christopher J. *Kant and the Creation of Freedom: A Theological Problem.* Oxford: Oxford University Press, 2013. Chapters 8-10.

On wider difficulties Kant has in relating divine action and human freedom, in relation to fall, grace, and atonement:

Firestone, Chris L., and Nathan Jacobs. *In Defense of Kant's Religion.* Bloomington: Indiana University Press, 2008.

Mariña, Jacqueline. "Kant on Grace: A Reply to His Critics." *Religious Studies* 33.4 (1997): 379-400.

Michalson, Gordon E., Jr. *Fallen Freedom: Kant on Radical Evil and Moral Regeneration.* Cambridge: Cambridge University Press, 1990.

———. *Kant and the Problem of God.* Oxford: Blackwell, 1999.

Wolterstorff, Nicholas. "Conundrums in Kant's Rational Religion." In *Kant's Philosophy of Religion Reconsidered.* Edited by Philip J. Rossi and Michael Wreen. Bloomington: Indiana University Press, 1991. Pp. 40-53.

Chapter Eight

On Kant's account of autonomy:

Ameriks, Karl. *Kant and the Fate of Autonomy: Problems in the Appropriation of the Critical Philosophy.* Cambridge: Cambridge University Press, 2000.

Engstrom, Stephen, and Jennifer Whiting. *Aristotle, Kant, and the Stoics: Rethinking Happiness and Duty.* Cambridge: Cambridge University Press, 1996.

Irwin, Terence. "Continuity in the History of Autonomy." *Inquiry: An Interdisciplinary Journal of Philosophy* 54.5 (2011): 442-59.

Kain, Patrick. "Self-Legislation in Kant's Moral Philosophy." *Archiv für Geschichte der Philosophie* 86 (2004): 257-306.

Korsgaard, Christine M. *Creating the Kingdom of Ends.* Cambridge: Cambridge University Press, 1996.

———. *The Sources of Normativity.* Cambridge: Cambridge University Press, 1996.

———. *The Development of Ethics: A Historical and Critical Study,* vol. 3: *From Kant to Rawls.* Oxford: Oxford University Press, 2009.

O'Neill, Onora. *Constructions of Reason.* Cambridge: Cambridge University Press, 1989.

Rawls, John. *A Theory of Justice.* Cambridge, MA: Harvard University Press, 1971.

Schneewind, J. B. *The Invention of Autonomy.* Cambridge: Cambridge University Press, 1998.

Sensen, Oliver, ed. *Kant on Moral Autonomy.* Cambridge: Cambridge University Press, 2013.

Stern, Robert. *Understanding Moral Obligation: Kant, Hegel, Kierkegaard.* Cambridge: Cambridge University Press, 2013.

Ward, Keith. *The Development of Kant's View of Ethics.* Oxford: Blackwell, 1972. Chapter 7.

Wood, Allen W. *Kantian Ethics.* Cambridge: Cambridge University Press, 2008.

———. *Kant's Ethical Thought.* Cambridge: Cambridge University Press, 1999.

Treatments of Kant's moral philosophy in relation to Thomas Aquinas:

Hinton, Timothy. "Kant and Aquinas on the Priority of the Good." *Review of Metaphysics* 55.4 (2002): 825-46.

Insole, Christopher. "A Thomistic Reading of Kant's *Groundwork of the Metaphysics of Morals:* Searching for the Unconditioned." *Modern Theology* 31.2 (2015): 284-311.

Glossary of Terms

All these concepts are explained when first used in the text, but I reproduce the explanations here, in case it may be helpful to refer to them when the concepts are used again later on in the book without the explanation being repeated. I list the concepts alphabetically. These are not intended to be water-tight, uncontroversial, or widely generalizable "definitions," but are brisk and partial explanations, sufficient to the task at hand of understanding an aspect of Kant's thought. In each case, the qualification "as used here, in the context of this book" should be considered to be inscribed in bold alongside the explanations.

Absolute spontaneity: a term used by Kant to describe a **non-compatibilist** conception of freedom, which he begins to reach out toward from the 1760s onward.

Alien/external cause: a cause that violates the freedom of the creature.

Autonomy: giving oneself *(autos)* the law *(nomos)*. Everything turns on who the "self" is who gives the law, and what the "law" is that is given. In chapter eight, I argue that the "self" is the **noumenal/intelligible self**, and the "law" is reason. At the core of "reason" is the project of acting for an end, rather than being determined by a cause. So the **noumenal self** gives to itself the project of end-setting as such: not because it is this or that end, or this particular person's end.

Christianized Platonist: someone who thinks that there must be a deep-structuring mind behind all things, which mind must have both understanding *and will,* because at the heart of all that is, is a free action of creation. This mind that grounds all possibilities is God.

Christian Platonist: someone with **Platonist** views, but who construes this commitment alongside, and after, assenting in faith to the classical doctrines of Christianity, such as creation *ex nihilo,* incarnation, trinity, grace, atonement, and concursus.

Compatibilism: the view that our being free is "compatible" with all the events in the universe being determined. The compatibilist would ask about an action: "did you understand what you were doing, and having understood it, did you want to do this action?" If the answer is "yes," the action is free, regardless of whether or not we were able to do otherwise, and of whether we are ultimately responsible for our actions. The early Kant (1750s-1760s) is compatibilist about freedom.

Concursus/concurrence: the conception of the "running together" of divine and human action, whereby God not only creates things *ex nihilo,* and conserves them in existence, but also acts directly and immediately in all of their actions, without violating the integrity or freedom of the creature. For divine and human action to "concur," the following conditions must be satisfied:
- God must act immediately and directly in the action of the creature.
- Neither God's action nor the creature's action would be by themselves sufficient for that action to occur.
- Neither action would exist in the absence of the other.

Critical thought: Kant's philosophy after around 1770, when he intended to tighten up on irresponsible knowledge claims.

Divine freedom: involves God perfectly expressing the divine nature, and being ultimately responsible for God's actions (there are no "external" factors acting upon God). It does not involve, though, God's being able to do other than the good, where goodness itself is an aspect of the divine nature.

Empirical realm/reality: the whole of what appears to us, mediated through the way in which we receive the world, that is, through space and time. Kant also calls this the **phenomenal realm**.

Epistemology: the theory of knowledge. A reflection on the various textures of assent that we give or withhold to propositions, including knowledge, belief, acceptance, and faith.

Essence: the "what-it-is-ness" of something, which gives this thing its fundamental order and nature. For example, what is the "essence" of the cat? It is "cat-ness": that which makes it what it is, inasmuch as it is a cat.

External/alien cause: a cause that violates the freedom of the creature.

Form/essence: the "what-it-is-ness" of something, which gives this thing its fundamental order and nature. For example, what is the "essence/form" of the cat? It is "cat-ness": that which makes it what it is, inasmuch as it is a cat.

Freedom: see **Divine freedom, Compatibilism, Human freedom in Kant's early thought, Human freedom in Kant's mature/critical thought, Non-compatibilism.**

Happiness: The state of a rational and free being who follows the moral law, and in the whole of whose existence everything goes according to her (rational, universalizable, and harmonious) wish and will.

Highest Good: where the moral law is obeyed (the "supreme condition"), and where, as a consequence but not an incentive, those who follow the moral law are proportionately happy (the "complete good").

Human freedom in Kant's early thought: a compatibilist conception, where our being free is "compatible" with all the events in the universe being determined. The compatibilist would ask about an action: "did you understand what you were doing, and having understood it, did you want to do this action?" If the answer is "yes," the action is free, regardless of whether or not we were able to do otherwise, and of whether we are ultimately responsible for our actions.

Human freedom in Kant's mature/critical thought: a non-compatibilist conception, where our being free is not compatible with all the events in the universe being determined. To be free, we must be able to do other than we do, and we must be ultimately responsible for our actions.

Intellectualism: the view that the structure of real possibilities depends upon the divine understanding/intellect.

Intelligible (or noumenal) selves: ourselves as we fundamentally are, outside of space and time, underlying the **phenomenal** appearance of ourselves in space and time.

Intelligible realm/world/reality: that which underlies all that appears to us. Reality at its most fundamental, from which all appearances are derived. Although the **phenomenal realm** depends upon the noumenal realm, the phenomenal realm as it appears to us does not resemble the noumenal realm. Kant also calls the intelligible realm the **noumenal realm/reality**.

Internal cause: a cause that does not violate the freedom of the creature.

Kingdom of ends: the community of **noumenal selves**, where everyone respects the project of end-setting, and the consequence is harmony and happiness.

Logical possibility: anything that does not involve a contradiction of the form "*a* and *not-a*," such as "the bachelor (= unmarried man) is married."

Metaphysics: the reflection on what is real. Not only the study of what sort of "physical" things might be real, but the study of everything that might be considered real (hence, that which comes "after" — although it can include — "physics"). A "metaphysical commitment to x" is a conviction that x is, in some sense, real.

Moral dependence (on God): the dependence that arises when God decides, through his will, to create something out of nothing, and to sustain it in existence.

Neglected alternative: the possibility that things-in-themselves might, for all we know, be spatial and temporal, and so determined.

Non-compatibilism: the view that our being free is not compatible with all the events in the universe being determined. To be free, we must be able to do other than we do, and we must be ultimately responsible for our actions.

Non-moral dependence (on God): where something depends upon being contained in the divine understanding, rather than depending upon the free choice of the divine will.

Normative: a "normative" statement tells us what ought to be done, or what ought to be avoided.

Noumenal (or intelligible) selves: ourselves as we fundamentally are, outside of space and time, underlying the **phenomenal** appearance of ourselves in space and time.

Noumenal realm/reality: that which underlies all that appears to us. Reality at its most fundamental, from which all appearances are derived. Although the **phenomenal realm** depends upon the noumenal realm, the phenomenal realm as it appears to us does not resemble the noumenal realm. Kant also calls the noumenal realm the **intelligible realm/world** or **intelligible reality**.

Noumenon/noumena: that which underlies **phenomena**, and upon which **phenomena** are dependent. Fundamental reality, which could be quite different from how things appear to us.

Occasionalism: the view that God is the only source of real action in the universe. When it seems to us that x causes y, this is God willing that y happen on the "occasion" of x happening.

Ontology: the study of being *(ontos)*, of "what has being."

Original freedom: a term used by Kant to describe a **non-compatibilist** conception of freedom, which he begins to reach out toward from the 1760s onward.

Phenomenal realm/reality: the whole of what appears to us, mediated through the way in which we receive the world, that is, through space and time. Kant also calls this the **empirical realm** reality.

Phenomenon/phenomena: that which appears (to us), either to our ordinary sense-perception, or to our scientific observations.

Pietism: a religious movement influenced by Luther, which emphasized the value of personal devotion, which devotion could be manifested by powerful emotive states and by practical ethical actions. Kant's childhood formation was in a Pietist home.

Platonist: someone who thinks there must be a deep and intelligible structure behind all things, of which the world that we know is a derivative appearance.

Practical reason: reason applied to the question "what should I do?" in relation to acting or making.

Real possibility: the way in which things can fundamentally be.

Substance: a finite entity capable of having properties. The "cat is black": the cat is the "substance," the blackness the property.

Theosis: the process whereby the human being participates in divinity, and takes on aspects of divinity, by virtue of divine action.

Theological rationalism: a dominant tradition of philosophical theology in eighteenth-century Germany, characterized by strong **Platonic** themes, and a conviction that reality is undergirded by uncreated essences contained in the divine mind. Alongside this metaphysical commitment is the epistemological conviction that reason can provide some sort of access to fundamental reality.

Theoretical reason: reason applied to the question "what can I know?" Also called **speculative reason**.

Thing-in-itself/transcendental object: fundamental **noumenal** reality, which underlies appearances.

Transcendental freedom: a term used by Kant to describe a **non-compatibilist** conception of freedom, which he begins to reach out toward from the 1760s onward.

Voluntarism: the view that the structure of real possibilities depends upon the divine will *(voluntas)*.

Index